The Word Disclosed

The Word Disclosed

John's Story and Narrative Preaching

by Gail R. O'Day

CBP Press

St. Louis, Missouri

Library of Congress Cataloging-in-Publication Data

O'Day, Gail R., 1954-
    The Word disclosed.

    1. Bible. N.T. John—Criticism, interpretation, etc.   2. Bible.
N.T. John—Homiletical use.
    I. Title.
BS2615.2.029   1987   226'.506   86-24510
ISBN 0-8272-4219-0

For William A. Beardslee
in gratitude for
his quiet strength
and
gentle wisdom

Contents

Foreword

The Fourth Gospel has a hard time at the hands of interpreters. Because the narrative is so elusive in its particularity, it
invites excessive fantasy on the part of expositors and excessive
speculation on the part of scholars. The outcome is that much of
our interpretation of the Fourth Gospel is in fact an imposition
from the outside, wherein the Gospel narrative is made to serve
concerns other than its own.

More recent methodological developments in literary criticism provide an alternative to such distorting imposition. But the
use of such newer methods requires not only literary finesse but
theological sensitivity. The rare combination essential to reading
the Fourth Gospel is powerfully evident in this work of Gail R.
O'Day. She exhibits the patience to follow the teasing, suggestive
idiom of the Gospel, which refuses our conventional analysis and
refutes our scholastic modes of certitude. She shows in inescap-
able ways that the way of speech in the Fourth Gospel is utterly
congruent with, and in the service of, the substance of the Word.
Where that way of speech is ignored (as it usually is), the substance of the Word will be missed (as it mostly is).

The elusive style, O'Day shows, is intentional, skillful, and
crucial to our reading, for it serves the liberated, liberating Word
who is Jesus. For the Fourth Gospel, Jesus is not that liberated,
liberating one except through the offer of this speech. Our usual
critical categories cannot "hold" the meaning of the text anymore
than obtuse, resistant faith can "hold" Jesus, who will be free and
on the move.

This book will not only give preachers some new sermon
ideas, though it will do that. It will invite to a new way of reading

7

8

and listening, a way of speaking that shatters old closed worlds and makes new worlds possible, "fresh from the Word." Ours is indeed a closed world—theologically, morally, politically. This book proposes a way to "un-close" that world by means of dis-closure. It is a demanding book. But this dis-closing is a demanding vocation, urgent for those who celebrate and trust the disclosure of John, and the Disclosed One who still gives new identity and fresh life. Preachers and congregations who fully appropriate this book will be led to a fresh sense of the authority of scripture and to fresh energy for faith in the world.

Walter Brueggemann
Columbia Theological Seminary

Preface

The task of preaching a Fourth Gospel text is often the true test for a preacher, because the Fourth Gospel texts are so different from what we have come to expect Gospel texts to be like. Very few of our "beloved" Jesus stories are found in the Fourth Gospel, and rarely do we quote the words of the Johannine Jesus in our teachings. It is the Jesus narrated by Matthew, Mark, and Luke whom the church meets most regularly in story, song, and worship. Preaching texts from the Synoptic Gospels, not John, are the mainstay of a preacher's repertoire. Yet the early church did not pass on to us only the Synoptic portraits of Jesus as authoritative for our lives and faith. The early church held the Johannine portrait to be canonical as well, and that fourth portrait therefore must also be attended to as authoritative and life-giving. Fourth Gospel texts do not appear in our lectionaries with much frequency, but when they do appear, the challenge to the preacher is to allow that "other voice" of Jesus to be heard.

This book is a series of exegetical reflections on the Fourth Gospel texts that are part of the Lenten lectionary for Year A. The book concludes with a brief interpretation of the Easter Sunday text for Year A, also from the Fourth Gospel. Each of the chapters is written with a view toward preaching these Johannine texts at their given place in the liturgical calendar. The book is not intended primarily as a lectionary guide, however, although it does serve that purpose. Its intent is broader than that. The aim of this book is to provide fresh access to the Fourth Gospel, for pastor and congregation alike, so that Johannine texts that frequently seem so elusive and frustrating to the preacher may more fully become a part of the vital life of the church. The Johannine

Jesus speaks powerfully to us, and if we can attune our ears to listen to the particular cadences of the Fourth Gospel, then our preaching from that Gospel will be empowered and empowering in new ways.

I have followed the translation of the Revised Standard Version. I have varied slightly from the Revised Standard Version at certain points in order to avoid unnecessary exclusive language. These variations are not significant enough, however, to warrant separate identification as "author's translation."

Several of these chapters were used as lectures for the Committee on Uniform Series, National Council of Churches, and for the United Church of Christ, Ohio Conference Annual Convocation for Church Professionals. I want to thank all the pastors and church professionals who attended the Ohio Convocation for their warm response and willingness to enter into dialogue around these Johannine texts. I want especially to thank Dr. Thomas E. Dipko, Conference Minister of the Ohio Conference, for his generous hospitality and enthusiasm for these lectures.

Three people have each contributed to this book in quite distinct ways. First, Walter Brueggemann, now of Columbia Theological Seminary, was my main theological and exegetical conversation partner during the writing of this book. His passion for the gospel and for life and scholarship shaped by the gospel helped me to find eyes to see and ears to hear. My indebtedness is great. Second, Herbert H. Lambert, editor of CBP Press, initially pursued the idea of this manuscript with me and encouraged me to put my ideas into print. The writing of this manuscript coincided with a period of great personal tragedy for him, and I am thankful to Herb for his continued interest in the project. Finally, I want to thank Donna Bass for the care with which she typed the manuscript. She met every revision with humor and forbearance.

This book is dedicated to my teacher, William A. Beardslee. It may be sheer folly to think that I can even begin to give back to him all that he has given me and taught me, but in dedicating this book to him, I make one small effort in that direction.

Gail R. O'Day
Eden Theological Seminary
The Feast of the Nativity
of St. John the Baptist, 1986

Introduction

The purpose of this study is to investigate how biblical texts communicate and how we communicate biblical texts. In a specific New Testament context, we want to ask how we encounter Jesus in the Gospel texts and how we can most appropriately and faithfully communicate the Jesus of these texts. Our questions therefore move in two directions: (1) How are we led and drawn *into* the text; and (2) How do we lead and draw *out* what we discover in the text?

There is a tendency in the contemporary church situation to reduce biblical stories to a central point, a thesis, or one pivotal teaching. This manner of handling the biblical texts seems both to assume and suggest that once we arrive at this central kernel of the text, we have correctly understood and appropriated the text. The paragraph and section titles that many translations of the Bible provide encourage a reductionistic reading of the text, because those titles seduce us into believing that they capture and communicate what the text is "about." The preacher, in particular, falls prey to this tendency, as he or she often attempts to make clear to the congregation in ten to twenty minutes the message of the lessons for that particular Sunday. The manner in which passages for sermon texts are selected, seen most clearly in the lectionary cycles that neatly parcel out scripture into "manageable" units, encourages the impulse to determine succinctly what the text is "about" and to transfer that meaning to the congregation. With the more familiar lectionary selections, in particular the Gospel readings, the task of determining what the text is "about" becomes increasingly laborious and unfruitful, because preacher and congregation both already know what the familiar stories say.[1] When we approach the biblical texts with the discovery of the central or essential kernel predominantly in view, we sadly limit the possibilities that the biblical texts offer for proclamation.

11

We need to rethink the way we approach biblical texts and the way we understand the task of preaching. The narrative texts of the Bible are more than just story lines that can be summarized, condensed, and paraphrased. When one reduces a biblical narrative to a simple story line or a single emphasis, the speaker may still be telling a *story*, but he or she will no longer be proclaiming the *biblical* story. Such summary and paraphrasing of the biblical story preclude any genuine engagement with the biblical text, because such summary and paraphrasing place us in the domain of abstractions, generalities, and propositions, and that is not the domain of the Bible and biblical faith.[2]

When we approach a biblical narrative, we need to ask ourselves if what we think we know about the story and its message prevents us from coming into direct contact with the text and from engaging with the particularities of that text as the subject of proclamation. We need to ask ourselves if we move too quickly away from the text itself, from what the narrative does, how the story flows, and focus instead on some outline of the events, some central point, on what the text is "about." Questions such as these invite us to take a closer look at the the text itself, to linger with the text, because these questions do not ask simply *what* the biblical story says, but *how* it says it. The theatre provides a helpful parallel in understanding this relationship between the *what* and the *how* of the biblical text. When we go to the theatre, we may already know the content of the play, but each performance allows the play to be heard anew.

The way that biblical stories are told, therefore, is neither gratuitous nor expendable. We need to take the *mode* of biblical storytelling seriously, because the promise for the renewal and resurgence of biblical preaching rests in attentiveness to that mode. For example, we readily recognize that the New Testament narratives, particularly the Gospels, are composed of different literary forms and types of literary expression—miracle story, parable, pronouncement story, discourse, dialogue, proverb, etc. But how frequently do our sermons, both our preaching styles and content, reflect this diversity of biblical form and mode of expression? Instead of allowing the biblical text to shape our sermons, we frequently allow our sermon to shape the text, narrowing the text to good sermon material, to "what will preach" (an expression that echoes through the halls of every seminary).

When we allow the concerns and demands of the sermon to supersede the concerns and demands of the text, we articulate the questions and understand proclamation in reverse. The church or the preacher then controls the text and does not submit to the text in its proclamation. In order to proclaim the biblical texts faithfully, we must first allow ourselves to enter into the texts, to be shaped by the biblical stories, in all their diversity and rough edges, and then move from that participation in the text to proclamation. Such proclamation will be able to capture and communicate not simply the subject matter of the story, the "point" of the story, but also the dynamics of the story, the narrative mode of the story. Then our hearers are not *robbed* of the experience of the text, but are *transformed* by a genuine experience of the text.

Why such insistence on our participation in the text and on *how* the story is told? Because when we read biblical stories, it is impossible for us to arrive at a full experience and understanding of these texts unless we take seriously the narrative mode of these stories and allow our reading and interpretation of the text to be shaped by that mode. When we read the Gospels, we are not reading a sequence of propositions about Jesus, nor are we reading disembodied theological texts. Rather, we are reading stories in which narrative and theology are interdependent and inextricably intertwined. The way the Gospels tell their stories of Jesus is integral to that story. No Gospel portrait of Jesus exists without its distinctive narrative vehicle. To separate the two, biblical narrative and theology, is to miss the essence of the biblical text and to do a disservice to biblical faith.

Literary analysis of biblical texts, analysis carefully attuned to the particularities of the way each text is composed, is therefore not something superimposed on, external to, or alien to theological and pastoral appropriation of biblical texts. Literary analysis that takes the biblical texts most seriously (and therefore takes its own methods most seriously) must always attend to the integration of narrative mode and theological claim.[3] To speak again in specific New Testament terms, when we read the Gospels, we are reading texts in which the story of Jesus has been told in four different ways. The existence of four different Gospels does not indicate that four different "points" about Jesus are being made, but that *four different stories about Jesus are being told.* We must be sensitive to and shaped by the way these four different stories are told. We cannot talk about the Jesus of the Gospels without talking about these different narrative modes, but neither can we talk about the different narrative modes of the Gospels without talking about the Jesus they present. This twofold realization has important implications for how we preach.

Thus far, I have spoken only in general terms about our tendency to preach around the distinctive character of biblical texts and the need to allow our questions, our study, and our sermons to be shaped by and reflective of *how* the biblical stories are told. The specific implications of these general observations will be investigated by studying four major texts from the Gospel of John: the major dialogues and accompanying narrative in John 3, 4, 9, and 11. These four narrative texts—Jesus and Nicodemus, Jesus and the Samaritan woman, Jesus and the man born blind, Jesus and Mary, Martha, and the raising of Lazarus, are very well-known stories. They are part of the Lenten cycle for Year A. They also have a traditional place in the history of the church as Lenten preparatory texts for Easter baptism.

One need only look at the way in which the lectionary attempts to divide these texts into pericopae, however, to recognize that these Johannine texts present an immediate and direct challenge to the distillation method of appropriating texts. These four texts cannot be broken neatly into eight to ten verse units, because the Fourth Evangelist did not tell his stories that way. These Johannine texts cannot be distilled or reduced, which is perhaps why Fourth Gospel texts play such a relatively small role in the annual lectionary cycles. We frequently use Johannine texts that contain pithy sayings (John 3:16 being the quintessential example), but the Johannine texts themselves *as texts* do not play a central role in the liturgical life of the church.

I have intentionally described the four texts I will be considering in the same way—*Jesus* and Nicodemus, *Jesus* and the Samaritan woman, *Jesus* and the man born blind, *Jesus* and Mary, Martha, and Lazarus, because that is how the Fourth Evangelist has carefully and intentionally structured these texts. The focus of each of these texts is on Jesus: Jesus the teacher (John 3), Jesus the prophet (John 4), Jesus the healer (John 9), Jesus the life-giver (John 11). In more encompassing terms that resound throughout the Fourth Gospel, the focus is on Jesus the revealer, the sent one of God.

There are other events in these stories—the blind man is cross-examined by Pharisees, Lazarus is raised from the dead in front of a great crowd—but these events and miracles do not function the same way as miracles function in the other Gospels. In the Synoptic Gospels, we are told short, compact stories that report events of Jesus' ministry, be they healing, teaching, or exorcism. In the Fourth Gospel, however, as these four texts show, we almost never have similar compact story units with taut narration of events. Instead, we have long dialogues in which event and discourse are completely intertwined. No one aspect of the story stands in isolation, but all are part of the dynamic of the narrative mode, a dynamic that focuses on who Jesus is and how he encounters us.

It is this *dynamic*, the intertwining of event and discourse, the involved interaction between Jesus and his dialogue partners, that we lose when we attempt to handle these Johannine stories as if they were the shorter stories of the Synoptic Gospels. We lose the interrelationship of narrative mode and theological claim when we begin too rapidly to narrow these texts to what the stories are about. In such a narrowing, we bypass the way the stories move us along toward Jesus. By moving too quickly away from the text itself, we do violence to the Johannine narrative and deprive ourselves of the full experience of the Jesus whom John presents to us. The challenge to us as hearers, teachers, and proclaimers of these texts is to allow ourselves and *our* hearers to move with John toward Jesus.

The four Johannine narratives that are explored in this book, then, provide a good starting point for thinking about preaching in new ways. This book is not a "how-to" book on preaching—it does not provide sermon outlines, sermon starters, sermon summaries. Rather, this book is an exposition of four Johannine texts in ways that provide fresh access to them for preaching. If we allow the fullness of these texts to play upon our imagination, we may be able to hear them in new ways. If we are able to hear these texts in new ways, we may find that our Lenten preaching is genuinely transformed by the Jesus whom we encounter in these texts. Perhaps, through such transformed preaching, we shall all receive "grace upon grace" (John 1:16).

1

From the Comfort of Slogan to the Risk of Experience (John 3:1-15)

John 3:1-15, the exchange between Jesus and Nicodemus, is a well-known incident in the Fourth Gospel.[1] This relatively short scene could be (and has been) neatly and succinctly summarized and made to appear quite similar to those scenes in the Synoptic Gospels in which a Jewish religious authority comes to question Jesus. In John 3:1-15, Nicodemus, a Pharisee, comes to Jesus and states that he knows Jesus is a teacher who has come from God. Jesus responds to Nicodemus' claim to knowledge with a teaching that Nicodemus misunderstands. This misunderstanding highlights the differences between Jesus and the Pharisee.

This brief summary of the exchange between Jesus and Nicodemus is apparently straightforward, but John 3:1-15 is actually far from straightforward and is in fact subtle and dense. In the marked contrast between the plot summary and the text itself, we can begin to see that focusing on the reducible data of this text in order to produce a neatly wrapped story prevents us from capturing what is really at work in this text. If we focus primarily on the fact of a meeting between Jesus and a Pharisee or on one isolated teaching (John 3:3, for example), and try to understand this scene along the same lines as we would understand a pronouncement story in the Synoptic Gospels, we miss what John wants us to see and hear in this scene and consequently miss the Jesus who is narrated here.

We need to look at *how* John tells this story of Jesus and Nicodemus, how he moves the reader from character to character, from understanding to misunderstanding to understanding. The dynamics of this text are complex, and only when we pay careful attention to the narrative mode, to how the narrative pieces are held together, will we be able to discover what John is saying and doing and be able to share in and be transformed by his portrait of Jesus.

The Context of John 3:1-15

The context of John 3:1-15 provides an important clue about how to read and interpret this text. The scene between Jesus and Nicodemus is immediately preceded by a Johannine summary statement about the response of many in Jerusalem to Jesus:

Now when he [Jesus] was in Jerusalem at the Passover feast, many believed in his name when they saw the signs which he did; but Jesus did not trust himself to them, because he knew all people and needed no one to bear witness of humanity; for he himself knew what was in humanity (John 2:23-25).

These words establish a contrast between people's judgment and response to Jesus and Jesus' attitude toward and discernment of such response. The many who believe in Jesus' name believe because they have seen Jesus perform signs, but Jesus does not trust himself to such a response. The contrast between the two attitudes is brought out even more sharply in the Greek text, because the same verb, *pisteuō*, is used both for the people's acceptance of Jesus (v. 23) and Jesus' resistance to such response (v. 24).

How do these verses provide a clue for the interpretation of John 3:1-15? John 2:23-25 is not simply a statement about partial, inadequate, or incorrect faith. These verses run deeper and in more directions than that. They raise questions that touch at the most basic themes of who we are, how we know and believe, and who Jesus is. The distrust of Jesus in the face of the many people who believed in his name because of the signs they saw performed should be a warning to us in our efforts to interpret Jesus too readily and to respond to Jesus too easily. Do we not respond in ways that resemble the response of those who saw Jesus at Passover when we read the stories of Jesus for signs, when we read the stories for single, simple points and names with which to categorize and label Jesus? Are we not often guilty of preaching sermons based on signs instead of sermons based on the broader and perhaps more elusive, more demanding experience of Jesus? This is the word with which John 2:23-25 sends us into the dialogue between Jesus and Nicodemus: Do not be so sure that you know who Jesus is and who you are.

The juxtaposition of John 2:23-25 and John 3:1-15 also provides an important example of the ways in which the mode of the text informs our experience of the text. In the Johannine summary of 2:23-25, the Fourth Evangelist provides the reader with a distanced report of the interaction between Jesus and the crowd at Passover. The reader has only the Fourth Evangelist's summary account of what has transpired and of the quality and character of this transaction. The narrative does not provide the reader with her own experience of Jesus and this crowd who base their faith on signs. We are once removed from the experience of the text and our experience can only be in and through what the narrator explicitly tells us. The reader, therefore, is primarily an observer of the reported experience. The mode of narration of 2:23-25 does not invite the reader to participate in the text.

The reader's relationship to the text changes dramatically in the dialogue between Jesus and Nicodemus. In this text, the reader is given firsthand experience of one of the many who were impressed by the signs Jesus performed (cf. 2:23 and 3:2). The same themes raised by John 2:23-25, questions of belief, knowledge, and identity, are central to the dialogue with Nicodemus, but John 3:1-15 does not *state* these themes, it *embodies* them. What is a *report* in 2:23-25 becomes a shared *experience* in 3:1-15, as the dialogue enables the reader to participate in the questions of the nature of human response (cf. 2:23 and 3:2, 12), the contrast between human knowledge and Jesus' knowledge (cf. 2:25 and 3:2, 7, 9-11), and questions of human identity (2:25; 3:3-8) and Jesus' identity (3:13-15). The dialogue between Jesus and Nicodemus does not report on this exchange between Jesus and a Pharisee, providing the reader with a ready-made set of conclusions. Nor does it explicitly enumerate these themes and questions for the reader. Rather, these questions are all evoked by Jesus' presence in the text. The richness of John 3:1-15 allows the reader to encounter Jesus just as Nicodemus does. With this context in mind, we can now turn our attention to the dialogue.

The Text

The Fourth Evangelist carefully prepares the reader for the dialogue between Jesus and Nicodemus. John 3:1-15 opens with two important introductory features: who Nicodemus is and when he comes to Jesus. First, Nicodemus does not come to Jesus as a private citizen, as an anonymous anybody. Nicodemus is a man with impressive credentials: "There was a *man of the Pharisees*, named Nicodemus, a *ruler of the Jews*" (3:1, italics added). Nicodemus' name is carefully encircled by the credentials that establish his status—*who* Nicodemus is is determined by *what* he is. The literary structure of this verse, with its repetitive emphasis on Nicodemus' standing, makes it clear that Nicodemus does not come to Jesus as a man who stands on his own, but as a man who is surrounded by his community. Nicodemus, as the pointed repetition of his credentials shows, is not independent, but is dependent on and representative of human structures of authority.

Second, Nicodemus comes to Jesus "by night" (v. 2). In a Gospel that from its opening verses emphasizes the contrast between light and darkness (1:4-5), this reference to the time of Nicodemus' visit cannot be an incidental detail. The visit under the cloak of darkness strikes a discordant note with the description of Nicodemus' status in 3:1. As a Pharisee and ruler of the Jews, Nicodemus is a *public* figure, but he does not come to Jesus publicly. Nicodemus' night visit suggests that he wants to hide himself, and thus introduces a note of tension into the narrative.[2] That Nicodemus comes in darkness points to possible tension between Nicodemus and the community with whom his credentials so tightly link him, but also indicates possible tension between Nicodemus and Jesus. Nicodemus' night visit suggests that he is hedging his bets on all sides.[3]

In these introductory verses, then, the Fourth Evangelist simultaneously establishes and undercuts Nicodemus' identity. John 3:1 presents a powerful, authoritative public figure; 3:2a presents a man who comes to Jesus at night, thus rendering his public persona less visible and his self-assurance a facade. We are intentionally given mixed signals about who Nicodemus is, and are not sure what to expect from this character.

Nicodemus' first words reinforce the opening image of Nicodemus as the public religious figure. Nicodemus, in his public identity, addresses Jesus with dignity and respect, from one teacher to another: "Rabbi, we know that you are a teacher come from God; for no one can do these signs that you do, unless God is with that person" (v. 2). Nicodemus speaks as a religious authority, drawing on his knowledge of God to support his views. The link between Nicodemus and his community, which appeared to be weakened by Nicodemus' night visit, is reestablished here, because Nicodemus does not speak just for himself. His use of the first person plural ("we know") implies that he speaks also for those whom he represents. The tension between Jesus and Nicodemus that the night visit suggested also seems to disappear, for Nicodemus' acknowledgement of Jesus as a *teacher from God* is an important affirmation of Jesus by a *"ruler of the Jews."*

Yet, in the context of John 2:23-25, the reader knows that the basis for Nicodemus' affirmation is inadequate. Just like the people in Jerusalem to whom Jesus would not trust himself, Nicodemus' profession of Jesus as teacher from God is based on the evidence of signs. Will Jesus now trust himself to Nicodemus as he would not trust himself to the crowd (2:24)? Nicodemus' confident statement of who Jesus is ("we know . . .") is diminished by the reasons he offers for his knowledge ("for no one can do these signs . . ."). The Fourth Evangelist again simultaneously establishes and undercuts who Nicodemus is and what he says. The reader is left to wonder whether Jesus will accept Nicodemus' affirmation of him as a teacher from God or reject it.

Jesus' response to Nicodemus, however, once again jars the reader's expectation of the progress of the dialogue and dislodges any interpretive preconceptions. Jesus neither directly affirms nor denies Nicodemus' statements, neither directly accepts nor rejects Nicodemus' affirmation of him. Jesus does not say to Nicodemus, "Yes, you are right, that is who I am," but neither does he say, "No, you are incorrect, you do not know who I am." Instead Jesus responds with a teaching that returns the onus of interpretation and response to Nicodemus (and the reader). "If I am a teacher," Jesus' words seem to say, "then be taught by one of my teachings." The carefully balanced ambiguity requires the reader to engage in a decision.

Jesus responds to Nicodemus with the following words: "Truly, truly, I say to you, unless one is born from above/anew, one cannot see the kingdom of God" (3:3) (author's translation). This saying is well-known to all of us, and in fact, these words of Jesus are what is most frequently isolated and taken away from this scene between Jesus and Nicodemus. This verse has become a slogan and prooftext for an entire strand of contemporary Christian experience.[4] Yet, our level of familiarity with these words is not balanced by an equal level of understanding of its narrative function. The use of John 3:3 as a slogan *assumes* that we clearly and definitively understand the meaning of Jesus' saying, but, in actuality, the very words of this saying make such a succinct, precise reading impossible. In our conventional interpretation and application of this verse, we have lost the recognition that this saying is *supposed* to be misunderstood. By appropriating Jesus' words here as a slogan, we engage in more reductionism. We pretend to make clear what is deliberately elusive.

The hinge of misunderstanding in John 3:3 is the Greek word *anōthen*, which means both "from above" and "again." The Johannine Jesus quite intentionally superimposes both meanings here, but this intentional double meaning is lost in English translations of this verse.[5] Most English versions translate *anōthen* as "again," "anew," and at best supply the second meaning, "from above," as an alternative in the footnotes or textual apparatus (e.g., RSV and NEB). Yet such a technique inadequately captures the complex dynamics of this verse, because the translator(s) have decided for the reader that one meaning is primary and the other secondary when the narrator intends we should not choose between them. The reader is therefore denied the experience of deciphering and interpreting the double meaning, an experience inherent in the language of the text. Until we restore the intentional double meaning of *anōthen* to this verse, we will be unable to interpret Jesus' words correctly.[6]

Nicodemus understands only the one meaning of Jesus' words, "born again," and is therefore unable to make any headway in his conversation with Jesus. Because he is oblivious to the two levels of meaning in Jesus' expression, Nicodemus can only focus quite concretely on the literal meaning of "born again," and therefore protests that what Jesus calls for is physiologically impossible: "How can a man be born when he is old? Can he enter a second time into his mother's womb and be born?" (v. 4). On the level at which Nicodemus understands Jesus, his questions are perfectly logical and appropriate. "I am an adult," says Nicodemus, "and you and I both know it is impossible for me to reenter my mother's womb, so don't talk to me about being born *again*." The irony of Nicodemus' response lies in this logic, because his words are correct and incontestable on one level, but that level stands in conflict and tension with what Jesus intends by the expression to be "born *anōthen*." Nicodemus' inability to understand is not because he does not know Greek. His inability to understand is a theological problem, as is our replication of his misunderstanding.

It is worth noting that even with this example of Nicodemus and his misunderstanding before us in this text, we still cling tenaciously to a single-level interpretation of *anōthen*. Just as Nicodemus could only interpret "born again" on one level, our contemporary interpretation of that expression also reduces its range of meaning. We, like Nicodemus, may "know" so well what our own slogans mean, that we are depriving ourselves of the richness of Jesus' words. The irony of Nicodemus' response may be unwittingly operative in contemporary Christian response as well.

Jesus' response to Nicodemus in 3:5-8 underlines the irony of Nicodemus' response, while simultaneously indicating the correct way to interpret his words. Jesus' new words provide a fresh interpretation of being born *anōthen*: "Truly, truly I say to you, unless one is born of water and the Spirit, one cannot enter the kingdom of God" (v. 5). This verse closely parallels 3:3, with two changes. To be born *anōthen* is now spoken of as to be born "of water and the Spirit," and "see the kingdom of God" becomes "enter the kingdom of God." In both verses Jesus is speaking of basic changes in the human condition that must precede a new and full relationship with God. Who better to speak of such a redefinition of human identity than the one who "knew all people and needed no one to bear witness of humanity" (2:25)? Yet such a change is not simply a psychic readjustment of human nature, nor is it the physical rebirth that Nicodemus envisions. The new birth about which Jesus speaks is neither of these things, but also somehow encompasses them both—which is why the intentionally ambiguous *anōthen* is the word used to communicate this change. Our efforts to translate and interpret tend to a dualism that the narrative precludes. The new birth is total, not with reference to any "part."

Jesus repeats his original expression, "You must be born *anōthen*" in 3:7, and provides another interpretation of this expression through his use of the double image of spirit/wind (*pneuma*.) This second usage of a word with innate double meaning reinforces the sense that a simplistic, reductionist interpretation does not and cannot apply in this dialogue. The image of the wind/spirit touches at the boundary of what is tangible and intangible, controllable and elusive. As it is with the wind/spirit says Jesus, "so it is with every one who is born of the Spirit" (v. 8).

Jesus' words in 3:7 deserve careful attention as a guide in interpreting this dialogue. First, there is an important shift in personal pronouns in this verse, a shift that the English language masks. The opening words of verse 7 are directly addressed to Nicodemus, "Do not marvel (second person singular verb) that I said to you (second person singular pronoun)." But Jesus' concluding words include a more general audience—"it is necessary for you (second person plural pronoun) to be born *anōthen*." When Jesus speaks of the necessity of a transformed human existence in verses 3 and 5, he uses an impersonal expression, "If anyone. . . ." In 3:7, however, Jesus uses direct personal address that explicitly includes more than the single individual with whom he is engaged in conversation. Nicodemus came to Jesus speaking for more than just himself ("we know . . ."). Jesus' response also reaches beyond the limited setting of this dialogue to create a wider audience. Jesus' words are broadened to include all those whose adherence to slogans and predetermined categories blocks their reception of new birth and new life.

Second, Jesus' request in 3:7, "Do not marvel that I said to you, 'You must be born *anōthen*'", should help inform the reader's response to Jesus' words. Jesus' words in 3:5-8 suggest that instead of interpreting *anōthen* as Nicodemus does (and as we tend to do), by focusing narrowly on one level of meaning and thus remaining in resistant amazement, the reader needs to work with both meanings and understand both levels of meaning as feeding off one another. The reader is asked to follow Jesus' lead in interpreting "to be born *anōthen*," instead of remaining with Nicodemus. But it is no easy task to hold together two conflicting meanings in a single image. The image, to be born *anōthen*, like the new existence of which it speaks, is difficult to grasp and impossible to control. Is it any wonder, then, that Nicodemus' response is to ask Jesus, "How can this be?" (v. 9).

The reader can empathize with Nicodemus and his befuddlement. This Pharisee and the reader after him have been twisted and turned as together we, Nicodemus and ourselves, move through the complexities of this dialogue.[7] Yet, Nicodemus' question is precisely the response that Jesus cautioned against in verse 7. "Do not marvel," Jesus said, but Nicodemus cannot move past the point of consternation, amazement, and confusion.

Nicodemus' question in verse 9 is literally, "How is it possible for these things to happen?" Nicodemus' question raises one of the central concerns of the Bible, the question of possibility versus impossibility. Nicodemus either cannot or will not let go of his categories of the possible and the impossible in order to be open and responsive to the new categories with which Jesus addresses him. Biblical faith, beginning with the annunciation to Sarah in Genesis 18, proclaims that human categories of possibility and impossibility cannot be allowed to determine the range of God's possibility. Human categories of the possible result in barrenness, hopelessness, and death. With God, however, "all things are possible" (Mark 10:27; cf. Mark 9:23; 11:22-24; Jeremiah 32:17, 27).[8] What is possible with God, according to this text in John 3, is the promise of new life, but Nicodemus balks at the offer, much as Sarah laughed in Genesis 18:12.

In this dialogue with Jesus, Nicodemus has not allowed what he knows and what he considers possible to be reshaped by the encounter with Jesus. Nicodemus knows what criteria make one a teacher from God, he knows the logic of human birth and life, and he is secure and settled in such knowledge. His knowledge clashes with the alternative world presented by Jesus, but Nicodemus clings to his settled knowledge and his conventional world.[9] This question in verse 9 is the last word spoken by Nicodemus in this dialogue. He will not let go of the comfort of his own predictable world, even when the alternative is the "impossible" offer of new life.

Jesus' words in verse 10 ironically underscore the quality and extent of Nicodemus' knowledge. Jesus speaks to Nicodemus with a quick and penetrating irony that characterizes much of the dialogue of the Fourth Gospel, "Are you a teacher of Israel, and yet you do not understand this?"[10] The quickness and bite of Jesus' words jolt the reader. For a minute we blush for Nicodemus, smugly thinking, "He really nailed you with that one, Nicodemus," until it slowly dawns on us that perhaps we have been nailed, too. John 3:1-15 opened with Nicodemus confidently asserting that "we know that you are a teacher come from God" (italics added). But now Jesus turns that confident assertion back on Nicodemus and on the reader: "If you are a teacher, if you know, why don't you understand?" The issue of credentials, so deftly introduced by the Fourth Evangelist in 3:1, is given an ironic twist by Jesus. The credentials and position may define the man, but they do not guarantee true knowledge and understanding. If anything they seem to preclude true understanding.

The contrast between what Nicodemus confidently knows and what Jesus knows and teaches is brought out further by the remaining words of Jesus in the dialogue. The inadequacy of Nicodemus' knowledge and belief is highlighted in verses 11-12: "Truly, truly I say to you, we speak of what we know, and bear witness to what we have seen; but you do not receive our testimony. If I have told you earthly things and you do not believe, how can you believe if I tell you heavenly things?" Again, as in verse 7, the shift in personal pronouns is important. Jesus initially addresses himself specifically to Nicodemus (I say to you, [soi], second person singular pronoun). After that initial reference, however, all the remaining second person pronouns are plural. Nicodemus disappears from the dialogue. Jesus' words move beyond the particular case of Nicodemus to include all who have seen and heard. The second person plural pronoun includes the reader in this address.

With the disappearance of Nicodemus, the dialogue in some ways has moved full circle. Nicodemus came to Jesus speaking of what we know, not only of what he himself knew, and Jesus now also speaks of what we know in deliberate contrast with the "you" represented by Nicodemus. In the statements of Jesus in verses 11-12, the reader is told directly what he has experienced to this point in the dialogue—Nicodemus does not know, despite his claims to the contrary. And more decisively, ample opportunity for knowing has been presented to Nicodemus—"we speak," "we bear witness," "I have told you"—but Nicodemus has been unable to receive what has been offered. Nicodemus, as a teacher and ruler of Israel, knows who Jesus is, knows that Jesus is a teacher of God, but such knowledge proves inadequate in the face

of the direct encounter and testimony of Jesus. Dependence on
such knowledge prevents Nicodemus from receiving the gift of
new life and new possibilities that Jesus has to offer.
The dialogue comes to a conclusion in 3:13-15. In these verses
the reader is given insight into Jesus' identity and into what it
means to speak of Jesus as a teacher from God. Nicodemus
asserts that Jesus must be a teacher come from God, but it is
verse 13 that establishes the full meaning of that expression: "No
one has ascended into heaven but he who descended from
heaven, the Son of man." It is not enough to say, as Nicodemus
does, that God must be with Jesus in order for him to perform his
signs. The more radical truth, which the ascent/descent formula
highlights, is that Jesus is shaped by his intimate and ongoing
relationship with God. Nicodemus' words in 3:2 are not false, but
are only the half-truth, because he has no idea of the extent of
Jesus' relationship with God and the true nature of his identity.

Verse 13 establishes Jesus' identity on the basis of the ascent/
descent motif;[11] verse 14 focuses on the nature of the ascent: "And
as Moses lifted up the serpent in the wilderness, so must the Son
of man be lifted up." For the third time in this dialogue, we have a
word with a double meaning. "To lift up" translates the Greek
verb *hupsoō*, but in addition to "lift up," this verb also means
"exalt." John 3:14 is the first prediction of Jesus' Passion in the
Fourth Gospel, and the use of *hupsoō* is revealing of the Fourth
Evangelist's theology of the cross. The moment of lifting up on
the cross and the moment of exaltation are one and the same, and
it is in this moment that the pieces of Jesus' identity fall together;
it is in this moment that eternal life becomes possible and available to the believer (v. 15).

In verses 13-15 we find the means to interpret the expression,
"to be born *anōthen*." Verses 3-8 focus on the question of human
identity and on what is necessary for human participation in the
kingdom of God. John 3:13-15 shows that this question of
human identity must be informed by and can only be answered
by who Jesus is. The Son of Man must be lifted up, so that
"whoever believes in him may have eternal life" (v. 15). So that
whoever believes in him can have and know life in another form,
can be born *anōthen*. To be born *from above* is to be born *anew*
in the lifting up of Jesus on the cross, in the glorification of Jesus
on the cross (cf. 13:31). This is the change in human existence of

which Jesus speaks, a change which can neither be understood nor accomplished through human categories of spiritual and physical rebirth. It can only be accomplished in the cross. The point of origin for the one now born is with Jesus, not with ourselves.

Nicodemus does not recognize this. With his confident assertion of what he knows about Jesus (v. 2) and his resistance to anything that conflicts with or contradicts what he knows about human existence and identity (vs. 4-9), Nicodemus operates in reverse. He cannot move beyond the comfort of slogans. He insists on determining who Jesus is through his knowledge of who we are. But, as the dialogue shows, such an effort will not work. Nicodemus does not understand, does not receive, does not believe. We cannot determine who Jesus is, but *who we are* must be determined by *who Jesus is*.

Conclusion

In verses 11-15, Jesus speaks directly and the contrast between Jesus and Nicodemus becomes clear. These direct statements, however, only make an impact because of the reader's experience of and participation in the narrative. The reader starts with Nicodemus, agreeing that Jesus is a teacher from God, but the dialogue shows the reader that Nicodemus really has no sense of what it means to speak of *Jesus* as the teacher from God. "Teacher from God" is the correct category, but Nicodemus' confident assertion supplies the wrong content. What he thinks a teacher from God is does not adequately convey who Jesus is. The categories with which Nicodemus approaches Jesus need to be reshaped and reconstituted by the direct encounter with Jesus. The Fourth Gospel allows the reader to participate in this reshaping and reconstitution by providing space in its narratives and dialogues for the reader to enter the text, and through the text the reader can encounter Jesus for herself. Narrative does not render what is already known, but renders what is not known until it is rendered in that particular articulation. The narrative rendering in John 3:1-15 gives a newness to Nicodemus and to the reader that did not exist until that narrative moment. The preacher is called to render that newness again in the preaching moment.

The "how" of this scene between Jesus and Nicodemus, the narrative dynamic of the text, demonstrates that one cannot start the process of interpretation and proclamation at the end. One cannot, for example, on the basis of the more direct statements of 3:11-15, interpret this text by saying, "What Jesus wanted to tell Nicodemus is . . . ." *That is not how this text functions.* To present this text simply as a vehicle through which one transmits data is to ignore the radical transformation of categories and the reorientation that has gone on in this dialogue and for the reader. Yes, there is content, there is identifiable subject matter, but the transference of content is not the goal of this text. Such an understanding renders the text itself expendable. The "lesson" of 3:1-15 is not to be found in a few catchy phrases, but lies in the transformative experience of Jesus that the text makes available.

When preaching John 3:1-15, therefore, we must be careful that we do not approach the text like Nicodemus approaches Jesus, certain that *we know* what this text is all about. If we approach the text in that way, our sermons will miss the richness of the dynamics of this text. We must allow our preaching to be shaped by the give and take between Jesus and Nicodemus, by the questions and answers, the understanding and misunderstanding. As we have moved through the text with Nicodemus in his struggle to understand Jesus and what he offers, we have found that we cannot assume automatically that *we know* (3:2) the correct answer to the question, "Who is Jesus?" We find instead that we need to allow the Fourth Evangelist to help us discover who and what Jesus is through the narrative dynamics of the text. It is the same with our preaching. We must allow our listeners in turn to be shaped by the give and take between Jesus and Nicodemus. When we offer our listeners that experience, then they have the chance for their categories of the possible and impossible to be redefined. Without that chance, we remain bound by the comfort of Nicodemus' slogans, closed to the new life God offers through Jesus.

2

From the Comfort of Tradition to the Risk of Experience (John 4:4-42)

Nicodemus, as we have seen, is a man of some accomplishment. He is a Pharisee, a ruler of the Jews, and a teacher of Israel. He is a man of the establishment, a man with responsibilities, authority, and position. When he speaks, he speaks for more than just himself (3:2). Yet this same responsibility, authority, and position cannot guarantee him "success" in his conversation with Jesus. Nicodemus is so bound by the comfort and security of his credentials and slogans (see 3:1) that the new life that Jesus offers passes him by. What Jesus the teacher has to offer does not correspond to the categories out of which Nicodemus the teacher operates, but Nicodemus does not allow his own categories to be reshaped. His identity is determined by the categories of the ruling establishment of which he is a part, and he is not ready to abandon that identity for the risk of the experience of Jesus.

In moving from John 3:1-15 to John 4:4-42, the Fourth Evangelist moves the reader from the religious and social center to the religious and social periphery. The individual with whom Jesus converses in John 4 is at the opposite end of the social, political, and religious spectrum from Nicodemus. Nicodemus is a male, a member of the Jewish religious establishment, a pillar of the Jewish community. The Samaritan woman is female, one of the despised Samaritans, with a suspect personal history.[1] The scene shifts from Jerusalem, the seat of holiness, to Samaria, the seat of uncleanness. The one constant in these two radically diverse settings is the presence of Jesus and his offer of himself and of new life. Jesus was not falsely impressed by Nicodemus' credentials and position, and Jesus will not be falsely condescend-

ing toward the Samaritan woman's lack of credentials and position. The question for the Samaritan woman, as it was for
Nicodemus, is whether she will be willing to accept Jesus' offer.

The Context and Structure of John 4:4-42

Jesus' visit to Samaria occurs while he is in the midst of a
journey from Judea to Galilee (4:3). In 4:43, after he has spent
two days with the Samaritans in their city, Jesus will resume his
journey toward Galilee. The Samaritan narrative, therefore, is
framed by references to movement toward Galilee. This framing
points out to the reader that Samaria is an interruption in Jesus'
journey from Judea to Galilee and not part of his original itinerary. It is an interruption that could not be avoided, however; as
4:4 makes clear, "He had to pass through Samaria."[2]

The language of 4:4 is strong and direct. The necessity of this
sojourn in Samaria may simply reflect the geographical reality.
The shortest route from Judea to Galilee was to pass through
Samaria, although most Jewish travelers would pick an alternate
route rather than come in contact with the Samaritans. The
necessity of this sojourn in Samaria may also be theological,
however, in that Jesus was called to present himself to the Samaritans, to offer himself to those whom his society deemed
unworthy. The two ways of understanding the necessity of the
Samaritan sojourn are not unrelated to one another, because
Jesus may have been willing to accept the geographical necessity
of the most direct route out of a conviction of the theological
imperative of his presence among the Samaritans.

The Samaritan setting of John 4:4-42, then, is not an incidental detail. In John 3:1-15, Nicodemus, a pure child of the Jews,
will not receive Jesus on Jesus' own terms. In 4:44, after Jesus
leaves Samaria, the Fourth Evangelist comments on the dishonor
and rejection Jesus finds among his own people. In Samaria, by
contrast, among those whom Jesus' own people reject, Jesus is
received and confessed as Savior of the world (4:42). Among the
opening words of the Fourth Gospel, the Fourth Evangelist
writes, "He came to his own home and his own people received
him not" (1:11). That reality of hostile rejection by one's own
provides an ironic counterpart to the positive reception Jesus

finds in Samaria. The response of the Samaritan townspeople to Jesus is in many ways a fitting epilogue to the Nicodemus story, for it underscores that God's graciousness does not operate according to preconceived categories.

With this context in mind, it will be helpful to establish a structure for this long text. Afterwards we will be able to proceed to a detailed analysis.[3] John 4:4-42 consists of two blocks of dialogue: verses 7-26, Jesus and the Samaritan woman, and verses 31-38, Jesus and his disciples. The most involved and engaging dialogue is in verses 7-26. Framing these two sections are sections of introduction (vs. 4-6), transition (vs. 27-30), and conclusion (vs. 39-42). The structure of this chapter can thus be outlined as follows:

I.   Introduction: Arrival at the Well   4:4-6
II. Dialogue: Jesus and the Samaritan Woman 4:7-26
III. Transition: Return of the Disciples and
                 Departure of the Woman   4:27-30
IV. Dialogue: Jesus and the Disciples   4:31-38
V.   Conclusion: Jesus and
                 the Samaritan Townspeople   4:39-42

This outline reveals the complexity of this text when compared with the Nicodemus story. In the Nicodemus story, only two characters are involved, Jesus and Nicodemus, and the entire unit focuses on the dialogue between the two characters. The only movement in the text is Nicodemus' unheralded disappearance at 3:11. In John 4:4-42, however, the Fourth Evangelist has provided the reader with a much more involved text. Three different sets of characters interact with Jesus—the Samaritan woman, the disciples, and the Samaritan townspeople. Not only are there more characters in this text, there is also considerable movement by these characters. The story narrates the arrival and departure of each set of characters from the well where Jesus is located (see 4:7, 8, 27, 28, 30, 40).

In the crush of the many characters who populate John 4:4-42 and the bustle of movement to and from the well, only one character remains constant—Jesus. Once Jesus arrives at the well in verse 6, he does not move from there until verse 40, when he goes to stay with the Samaritans in their city. John 4:4-42 is a carefully and elaborately constructed text, composed with narrative and literary intentionality. The stability of Jesus, highlighted by the continual movement of the other characters, is a mark of that intentionality. Jesus' reliable presence in the story is the Fourth Evangelist's way of affirming through narrative that "Jesus Christ is the same yesterday and today and for ever" (Hebrews 13:8). Much of the confusion of this story will abate if we keep our attention fixed on Jesus as we read and listen to this text. The interpretive task of the preacher is to help the congregation fix its attention on Jesus.

The scenes of introduction, transition, and conclusion are signs of the interweaving of narrative and dialogue in this text. The conversations between Jesus and the Samaritan woman and Jesus and his disciples are tightly embedded in their narrative context. The relationship between narrative and dialogue in the telling of this story must therefore be taken seriously. As with the Nicodemus text, John 4:4-42 also defies simple plot reduction and summary. One cannot rush to the "themes" of this text because the Fourth Evangelist has not provided us with a text through which we can rush. Instead the Fourth Evangelist has provided us with a text that invites the reader to enter into its world and to participate in the transformation of categories and experience wrought by Jesus. The challenge in preaching John 4:4-42 is to keep open the invitation to a new world that this text makes available.

The Text
Introduction: Verses 4-6

As noted, Jesus' visit in Samaria begins as an interruption in his original plans. The city in Samaria where Jesus finds himself, Sychar, is described to the reader in terms that immediately bring the Old Testament to mind—"near the field that Jacob gave to his son Joseph. Jacob's well was there . . ." (vs. 5-6). Jesus has not arrived at a history-less place, but rather at a place whose very location is defined by its relation to the patriarchal story. The story of Jesus is intentionally set by the Fourth Evangelist within the traditions and stories about Jacob.[4] The traditions that are introduced in these opening verses will take on more importance as the story of John 4:4-42 unfolds.

Jesus arrives at Jacob's well in the middle of the day and sits down beside the well, wearied from his journey (v. 6). The detail of verse 6 adds a touch of realism to the story, but it also provides a transition to the next section. Jesus' request for a drink of water in verse 7 makes perfect sense against the backdrop of his fatigue from the journey.

These opening verses, then, introduce several details that the rest of the text will develop. First, as mentioned earlier, they introduce the necessity of Jesus' presence in Samaria. As the reader moves through John 4:4-42, it will be important to remember that Jesus is not in Samaria on a whim but because of a conviction about his vocation. Second, the person of Jacob figures prominently in these opening verses. The ground for a comparison between Jesus and Jacob is set. The physical setting of this story, *Jesus* seated at *Jacob's* well, underscores the comparison between Jesus and Jacob. Third, Jesus' posture at the well is one of vulnerability and need. He is tired and sits to rest. In verse 7 Jesus will make his need known to the Samaritan woman. The reader must wait to see how the Samaritan woman will receive Jesus' act of vulnerability and whether she will reciprocate his openness.

Jesus and the Samaritan Woman
Verses 7-26

A Samaritan woman arrives at the well to draw water. The two central characters are now in place. Jesus begins the conversation with the woman with a request, expressed in the imperative: "Give me a drink" (v. 7). It is, on the surface, a simple enough request. Jesus is weary from his journey, it is the middle of the day (v. 6). He is alone and without refreshment because his disciples have gone into the city to buy food (v. 8). Like Elijah requesting food and drink from the widow of Sidon (1 Kings 17:10-11), Jesus interrupts a woman in the midst of her household work to request a gesture of hospitality. Unlike the widow of Sidon, however, who shared with Elijah from the little that she had, the Samaritan woman does not respond to Jesus' request with an offer of water. Instead she greets his request with stunned amazement and consternation: "How is it that you, a Jew, ask a drink of me, a woman of Samaria?" (v. 9a).

From the Samaritan woman's perspective, Jesus has violated two societal conventions in requesting water from her. First, as the narrator's comment in verse 9c makes explicit, Jews did not invite contact with Samaritans, since Samaritans were understood to be ritually unclean. Jesus, however, by accepting the necessity of traveling through Samaria, has already demonstrated his willingness "to have dealings with Samaritans." In requesting water from the Samaritan woman, Jesus shows himself to be independent of traditional Jewish customs and expectations, but the Samaritan woman cannot see that. She only sees a Jew senselessly violating tradition.

Second, the Samaritan woman also understands Jesus to be violating another deep-seated convention—that of male/female interaction. The woman's amazement that Jesus, a Jewish *man*, is speaking with her, a Samaritan *woman*, is echoed in the disciples' reaction when they arrive at the well in verse 27. A teacher should not engage in conversation with a woman, and especially not with an unknown woman in public.[5] There was no good reason for Jesus to be in conversation with this woman. By speaking with the woman, he violates both Jewish and Samaritan expectations.

The Samaritan woman is so taken aback by Jesus' violation of tradition that his need of hospitality is forgotten. No water is offered to the tired traveler. She is unable to respond to Jesus because his request violates the conventions and traditions around which she structures her life. She cannot move beyond Jesus' Jewishness (and his maleness) to respond to his vulnerability and need. She can only ask "how," much as Nicodemus could only ask, "How can this be?" in 3:9 (cf. 3:4 also).

The Samaritan woman has turned a simple request for water into a question of identity and an issue of social contrasts— Jewish identity versus Samaritan identity, male identity versus female identity. Perhaps to the reader's surprise, Jesus will continue the question of identity in his own remarks. He does not repeat his request for a drink, but instead probes more deeply into the question of who it is that is so bold to request water from the woman: "If you knew the gift of God, and who it is that is saying to you, 'Give me a drink,' you would have asked him, and he would have given you living water" (v. 10).

The woman's question of verse 9 has been exploded open. Jesus' words in verse 10 indicate that the woman was correct to draw attention to Jesus' identity, but that she really has no idea what she is asking. Jesus' words focus on her lack of knowledge: "If you knew. . . ." The Samaritan woman knows only that a Jew is asking her for water. What she does not know is that this "ordinary" Jew who stands before her is in reality the King of the Jews (19:19); that the Jew who asks her is in reality the one in whose name we may ask (14:14, 16:24).

In asking the Samaritan woman to identify who he is, Jesus is asking one of the central questions in the Fourth Gospel. We have already seen this question in the Nicodemus story. Nicodemus thinks the answer to the "who is Jesus" question is "a teacher from God," but John 3:1-15 shows that the question of Jesus' identity can only be answered by pointing to the cross. This identity question will also be central in the texts of John 9 and 11, which we will examine. Here in 4:10 Jesus explicitly raises this question, and the reader must therefore read John 4:4-42 carefully to see how the question is answered. By placing this question in Jesus' own mouth, the Fourth Evangelist signals its pivotal importance.

Jesus' words in verse 10, much like his words to Nicodemus in 3:5, move the conversation to a new level. Jesus greeted Nicodemus' acknowledgement that Jesus was a teacher from God with a teaching about new birth that moved the conversation beyond Nicodemus' expectations. In this text, Jesus greets the woman's words about Jews and Samaritans with words about the gift of God and living water. He offers an invitation to the woman, an invitation to new knowledge and to transformed life. The onus of responsibility falls on the woman, because Jesus can only offer, he cannot force her to receive. If she accepts the proffered invitation, if she can identify the gift of God and the identity of the one with whom she speaks, then a dramatic role reversal will occur, an unprecedented act of transformation. If she accepts the invitation, the woman will turn to Jesus in vulnerability and need, and he will give to her. She who was asked to give would be the one given to.

More than the woman's role is transformed, however. The water that is given is transformed, too. Jesus requested well water from the woman; he offers her "living water" (*hydōr zōn*). "Living water" can be understood in two ways. First, the expression can be understood as referring to spring water, that is, fresh, running water. But it can also be understood as referring to "living" water, that is, water brimming with life. Once again we find the Fourth Evangelist intentionally using words with a double meaning (cf. *anōthen*, *pneuma*, *hupsoō* in John 3), intentionally using the richness of language to push beyond conventional assumptions and expectations. The juxtaposition of "living water" with the "gift of God" leads one to suspect that Jesus is speaking of more than running water here,[6] but the Fourth Evangelist leaves all possibilities open. The ambiguity of the expression *hydōr zōn* is not resolved in verse 10, but is carried forward into the rest of the narrative.

The Samaritan woman's response in verses 11 and 12 indicates that she has not understood the nature of the invitation offered her by Jesus. He has offered her a transformed existence and living water, but the woman acts as if she has heard none of that. She is still back where she was at verse 9, focusing on the audacity of Jesus' request for drinking water. All she can hear is that this Jewish man who moments ago was requesting water for himself because he had no way to get any from the well (v. 11), is now foolish enough to offer her living water. The woman does not recognize the ambiguity of the expression "living water" and reacts solely on the level of drinking water. Just as Nicodemus heard only one level of the expression "to be born *anōthen*" and therefore responded to Jesus' offer with protests of logical and physiological impossibility; so too the woman responds with protests of logical and material impossibility. "Sir, you have nothing to draw with, and the well is deep; where do you get that living water?" (v. 11). The reader knows, as the woman does not, that Jesus and the woman are conducting their conversation on two quite distinct levels.

The woman's question in verse 11 is one of the most ironically charged questions in the Fourth Gospel, as she asks the origin of Jesus and his gifts.[7] Throughout the Fourth Gospel, the Fourth Evangelist contrasts people's misperceptions about the origin of Jesus and his gifts with the reality of his origin (e.g., 1:29; 3:8; 4:11; 6:5). In asking this "from where" question, the Samaritan woman has asked a question that is plausible for both meanings of "living water," but the irony of the question arises because the woman is only aware of the question's appropriateness in regard to the source of drinking water. She does not know that she has asked a question that could indeed enable her to answer the question Jesus asked her in verse 10. If she knew where the living water came from, she would also know who Jesus is.

The reader of the Fourth Gospel knows where Jesus and his gifts are from—they are from God (e.g., 3:35; 5:36; 7:29). Jesus himself is the ultimate gift of God, the one whom God gave for the world (3:16). The woman does not know this, however. She knows only that a Jew has violated convention by requesting water from her and is now making her an inappropriate offer of running water.

Verse 12 indicates that the woman thinks Jesus has done more than violate social conventions and logical expectations. His preposterous offer of water when he has nothing with which to draw is an affront to the traditions of Jacob. "Our father Jacob" was able to produce water from the well at Haran only by a miracle.[8] How could this strange Jew think he could produce living water? Is he "greater than our father Jacob"?

This question is a universally recognized instance of Johannine irony.[9] The source of its irony is easy to spot—for the Fourth Evangelist and his readers, Jesus was indeed greater than Jacob. The comparison between Jesus and Jacob which was anticipated in verses 5-6 is now made explicit. Again the woman's inability to penetrate Jesus' identity comes to the surface. She is so confident of her assessment of the situation, of who Jesus is, of how he stands in relation to Jacob, that she cannot see and hear what is offered her. Jacob gave "us" the well, he drank from it, his cattle drank from it. His whole household was refreshed by Jacob's gift of water. How could this tired, thirsty Jew possibly offer any water which could surpass the water offered by Jacob?

The woman has asked rather facetiously if Jesus is greater than Jacob (the interrogative particle *mē* with which the question begins indicates that the woman anticipates a negative response). Instead of answering her question directly and explicitly addressing his relationship to Jacob, Jesus moves the conversation back in the direction of verse 10. The woman wants to conduct the conversation on the level of deep wells and drinking water (vs. 9, 11, 12); Jesus wants to conduct the conversation on the level of the gift of God and water that springs up to eternal life (vs. 10, 13, 14). Jesus places his gift of water (vs. 13 and 14) next to Jacob's gift of water (v. 12), and invites the woman to choose. Will she choose the old water, which is abundant but does not quench thirst, or will she choose the new water, which wells up to eternal life? Verses 13 and 14 actually do answer the question asked in verse 12, but the woman must have ears to hear and eyes to see. Once again Jesus gives the woman the chance to answer her own question (cf. the words "If you knew . . . ," in verse 10).

The water that Jacob offered may have refreshed Jacob and his sons and his cattle, but "every one who drinks of this water will thirst again" (v. 13). The woman had cataloged all those who drank from Jacob's well as proof of the superabundance and magnitude of Jacob's miraculous gift. Jesus' words in verses 13 and 14 ironically undercut the woman's claim, however, by suggesting that even though there was enough water for all, the water offered by Jacob (and drunk by Jacob) could not satisfy thirst. Jacob's gift of water may have been miraculous and its copiousness legendary, but it could not assuage thirst and satisfy human need.

By contrast, "whoever drinks of the water that I shall give him will never thirst" (v. 14a). Jesus promises that those who drink from the water he gives will never thirst again. Jesus promises that human needs will be attended to, that thirst will be eradicated from the list of human fears. In a land in which drought is a frequent symbol of disorder and death (cf. Jeremiah 2:6; 14:1), the claim that Jesus makes for his gift of water is staggering. He reaches down to the most basic human needs and fears and offers newness and hope. In John 3, Nicodemus was offered the promise of new life, of being born *anōthen*. Now the Samaritan woman is also offered the promise of new life, because "the water that I shall give her will become in her a spring of water welling up to eternal life" (v. 14b). Jesus offers more than simple refreshment. He offers water that reorders and reshapes our lives, that gives us resources we did not have before this water was offered. This offer of water, however, requires that we end our fascination with and reliance on other wells (cf. Jeremiah 2:13).

That Jesus' words in verses 13 and 14 are words of hope can be seen even more clearly when we allow ourselves to hear the echoes of Second Isaiah that resonate in the background of these verses.[10] The contrast between water that quenches thirst and water that does not recalls the joyous poetry with which Second Isaiah concludes:

> Ho, every one who thirsts,
>   come to the waters;
> and he who has no money,
>   come, buy and eat!
> Come, buy wine and milk
>   without money and without price.
> Why do you spend your money for that which is not bread,
>   and your labor for that which does not satisfy?
> Hearken diligently to me, and eat what is good,
>   and delight yourselves in fatness (Isaiah 55:1-2).

According to this poem, life will no longer be dominated by systems and conventions that perpetuate vain hunger and thirst. Instead, life will now be lived so that food really nourishes and drink really refreshes—and the abundance of both is for all.[11] The promise made by Jesus in John 4:13-14 continues this promise of Second Isaiah, now embodied in the person and offer of Jesus.

In the history of interpretation of verses 10-14, two referents have been frequently supplied for "living water"—either the Spirit or the revelation carried by Jesus. In more recent scholarship, however, it has become increasingly apparent that it is not necessary to decide between the two.[12] The language of the Fourth Gospel is intentionally open enough to include both. In John 7:37-39, where the gift of living water is spoken of again, both Jesus (v. 37) and the Spirit (v. 39) appear to be the source of the offer of new life. The offer of new life is accessible through both the person and word of Jesus and the abiding presence of the Spirit. Both bear witness to the life-giving power of God that shatters all pseudo-sources of life. What matters is not a sharp delineation between the Spirit and the revelation carried by Jesus, but that the proffered gift of living water is embraced.

Again Second Isaiah offers guidance in the interpretation of these Johannine verses. In Isaiah 44:2b-4, God makes this promise to Israel:

> Fear not, O Jacob my servant,
>   Jeshúran whom I have chosen.
> For I will pour water on the thirsty land,
>   and streams on the dry ground;
> I will pour my Spirit upon your descendants,

and my blessing on your offspring.
They shall spring up like grass amid waters,
like willows by flowing streams.

These words of assurance and salvation are conveyed in images of the outpouring of water and Spirit that give new life (cf. John 3:5). Israel's fears are dispelled and hope is made available through God's gift of life-giving water. Jesus uses the same range of images in John 4:13-14 to dispel fear and evoke hope. Jesus offers water which, like the water of Isaiah 44:3a, will refresh the thirsty, but which also, like the Spirit of Isaiah 44:3b, carries with it blessing and promise. The blessing and promise of John 4:14 is of eternal life, the same promise made in John 3:15.

Is Jesus greater than "our father Jacob"? Neither Jesus nor the Fourth Evangelist answers that question explicitly. The Samaritan woman and the reader must ponder what Jesus offers and decide that question for themselves. In preaching this text, the preacher must allow the congregation to arrive at the same moment of decision, to sense for themselves what Jesus is offering and what is at stake in rejecting or accepting the offer. Jesus cannot make the decision for the Samaritan woman. He can only offer her living water and invite her to a transformed life. Similarly, the preacher cannot preempt the decision-making process for those to whom she preaches. The preacher can only offer the congregation living water and invite us to a transformed life. It is through the sermon that that offer and that invitation must be heard.

Will the Samaritan woman accept Jesus' invitation to new life, or will she stay where she is, embedded in the conventions and traditions to which she is accustomed? "Sir," she says to Jesus, "give me this water, that I may not thirst, nor come here to draw" (v. 15). The Samaritan woman's initial words to Jesus indicate that perhaps she has indeed heard him, that she understands the promise and power of living water. By the time she finishes speaking, however, we discover that the woman is still on the level of deep wells and drinking water. The woman is concrete operational. She squeezes his disclosure into her already established categories. She requests water from Jesus, just as he predicted in verse 10, but the transformation Jesus envisioned for her is incomplete. The woman still cannot answer the question of Jesus' identity, and because of that, she does not fully understand what it is that Jesus offers and that she requests. Her lack of understanding is partly cognitive, but is also religious obduracy.

The Samaritan woman's final words in verse 15, that she may not "come here to draw," indicate that she is still concerned with miraculous drinking water and not with living water that transforms human needs and fears. The woman understands the offer of water to be related to a particular well or spring, and not to the person and presence of Jesus. Nicodemus could not comprehend what it meant to be born *anōthen* because he could not move beyond the physiological limitations of his mother's womb. So, too, the Samaritan woman cannot comprehend living water because she cannot move beyond the familiar wells and water jars that her categories control and administer. She cannot understand because everything is already explained. In one respect, however, the Samaritan woman has moved beyond Nicodemus. Even though she does not fully understand, she at least is open to Jesus' invitation and asks him to give to her. As we shall see again when we discuss John 9, openness to Jesus is a critical beginning place for the risk of the experience of Jesus.

The request for water in verse 15 brings the first half of the conversation between Jesus and the Samaritan woman to a close. Verse 10 set the agenda for this first half: "If you knew . . . you would have asked," and the Samaritan woman, as noted, has only been partly successful. She has asked, but she has asked without knowing who Jesus is. When Jesus speaks to the woman again in verse 16, it will no longer be about living water. He will turn the conversation in a new direction that will attempt to provide another point of access to the question of Jesus' identity.

Verses 16-19 have received the most controversial treatment of any of the sections of this long chapter. The majority of interpreters, scholars and preachers alike, tend to focus almost singlemindedly on the woman's "sinfulness" and her "shady past."[13] Such interpretations, however, do a great disservice to this dialogue between Jesus and the Samaritan woman. When we read verses 16-19 carefully, we notice that the history of the woman's five husbands is presented quite disinterestedly, with no suggestion or coloring of moral outrage or judgment. How or why the woman has had five husbands and what the quality of those marriages was is not a concern of the Evangelist as he tells the story. More importantly, those questions are also unimportant to

Jesus. One searches in vain for any words of judgment about the woman's character uttered by Jesus in these verses. This exchange between Jesus and the Samaritan woman is not an attempt to bring the woman face to face with her sinfulness or to place her in a posture of confession before Jesus. To see the text in this way is to miss the main function of the exchange. The conversation of verses 16-19 is intended to show the reader something about Jesus, not primarily about the woman.

This new piece of conversation opens with another request by Jesus. In verse 7 he requested a drink; now he requests that the woman summon her husband and return to the well (v. 16). The woman did not comply with Jesus' first request because it was impossible according to her customs and conventions. She will not comply with Jesus' second request either, because it, too, is "impossible." She has no husband (v. 17). Jesus, as we have seen already in John 3, does not take impossibilities at face value, however. He takes the woman's refusal and turns it back on her: "You are right in saying, 'I have no husband'; for you have had five husbands, and he whom you now have is not your husband; this you said truly" (vs. 17-18).

Jesus begins and ends his speech by asserting that the woman has spoken truthfully. Yet within the frame of these two affirmations, Jesus places the woman's "truthful" statement in an unexpected context. Jesus has been able to penetrate beyond the surface level of the woman's words and arrive at the truth about the woman's life. Jesus moves beyond the conventional reading of "I have no husband" to its surprising truth. For the woman— and the reader—Jesus' ability to see and to know is stunning. Jesus' perception is stunning to the woman, because Jesus has seen through her understatement to the truth. Jesus' perception is stunning to the reader, because the reader had accepted the woman's words at their conventional face value, and had no hint of the surprising truth uncovered by Jesus. The woman has indeed spoken the truth, but the reader is unable to discover that truth without Jesus' assistance.

It is no wonder, then, that Jesus' insight into the woman's words and life leads her to declare him to be a prophet (v. 19). The woman's response recalls the response of Nathanael in 1:47-49. Jesus recognizes Nathanael as "an Israelite in whom there is no guile," simply by virtue of having seen Nathanael under the fig tree. Jesus' recognition of him leads Nathanael to declare Jesus to be the Son of God and the King of the Jews. With both Nathanael and the Samaritan woman, a demonstration of perception and insight on Jesus' part leads to a christological confession. An important difference between the two scenes, however, is that the reader can only observe Jesus' demonstration of knowledge with Nathanael (cf. also the passive role of the reader in 2:23-25), whereas in 4:16-19 the reader experiences the unveiling of that knowledge for himself. The reader shares in the stunning recognition of Jesus' ability to know.

Against the backdrop of her confession of Jesus as a prophet, the Samaritan woman places before Jesus the critical issue in Samaritan/Jewish relations: What is the proper place of worship, this mountain (Gerizim), or Jerusalem (v. 20)? In one sense the woman returns to her initial comment of verse 9, which also focused on the relationship between Samaritans and Jews. She no longer broaches the question in consternation and disbelief, however. Instead she turns for instruction to someone she perceives to be a prophet.

This move on the woman's part is not, as is frequently argued, an act of distancing, an effort to extricate herself from an embarrassing conversation. Such a view of verses 20-26 is based on a misperception of the function of verses 16-19 and on an excessive devaluation of the woman as a legitimate conversation partner.[14] By asking Jesus about the proper place of worship, the woman is not disengaging from Jesus because she is afraid to have her "sinfulness" probed more deeply. Rather, her inquiry about worship is an act of engagement with Jesus, because she anticipates that Jesus, as a prophet, will be able to speak an authoritative word. In acknowledging Jesus as a prophet and turning to him for instruction, the Samaritan woman takes a decisive step toward fulfilling the "If you knew . . ." condition of verse 10. The exchange between Jesus and the woman in verses 20-26, with the focus on worship, may bring her even closer to discovering Jesus' full identity. Her courage in asking Jesus means she risks her whole tradition to a Jew.

When the Samaritan woman asks Jesus about worship, she speaks to him in very traditional categories—our fathers versus you, this mountain versus Jerusalem. Jesus' response picks up the woman's traditional categories: "Woman, believe me, the hour is coming when neither on *this mountain* nor in *Jerusalem* will you worship the Father. *You* worship what *you* do not know; *we* worship what *we* know, for salvation is from *the Jews*" (vs. 21-22, italics added). He does not stay bound by those traditional categories, however. Jesus utilizes the language of "you" (Samaritan) / "we" (Jews) and "this mountain"/ Jerusalem not to confirm tradition, but to transcend it. The answer that Jesus provides the woman as to the proper place of worship explodes all traditional categories, both Samaritan and Jewish, by focusing on the power of eschatological newness and the true nature of worship. Jesus shatters her categories, but by dismissing Jerusalem as well, also shatters his categories and those of the Jews.

The key to Jesus' superseding of traditional categories lies in the phrase, "The hour is coming, and now is" (v. 23). "The hour is coming" (see also v. 21) is a word of promise and anticipation. The phrase "and now is" signals that this anticipated time of promise and hope is upon us. Through this impingement of God's full hope, true worship will no longer be defined by place or ethnicity. Instead "true worshipers will worship the Father in spirit and truth, for such the Father seeks to worship him. God is spirit, and those who worship him must worship in spirit and truth" (vs. 23-24). Both "this mountain" and Jerusalem lose their status as holy places, because God's presence will neither be defined nor limited to the sanctuaries managed and legitimated by the tradition.[15] God's presence will not be fixed and located in terms of a place, because God is Spirit. God moves freely (cf. John 3:8) and seeks those who worship freely in spirit and truth.[16]

Jesus' words to the woman in verses 21-24 signal the inbreaking of the new age. "The old has passed away, behold, the new has come" (2 Corinthians 5:17; cf. also Isaiah 43:18-19; 66:17). At the very beginning of the Fourth Gospel, the Fourth Evangelist pointed toward this eschatological transformation of the traditional: "For the law was given through Moses; grace and truth came through Jesus Christ" (1:17).[17] It is Jesus' very presence that changes the word of anticipation—"the hour is coming," to a word of inbreaking—"and now is." The grace and truth that come through Jesus make possible worship in spirit and truth. A new form of worship means a new form of obedience and life. The old categories and traditions cannot contain the richness and fullness of what has been received from Jesus (cf. 1:16).

The Samaritan woman's response in verse 25 indicates that she has picked up on the eschatological tone of Jesus' words: "I know that the Messiah is coming (he who is called Christ); when he comes, he will show us all things." Jesus speaks of the coming hour; the woman speaks of the coming One. The critical difference between Jesus' words and the woman's words, of course, is that the woman disregards the eschatological immediacy so central to verses 21-24. The woman's words reflect nothing of the "and now is" of which Jesus speaks. To Jesus' vision of eschatological newness, the Samaritan woman responds with traditional eschatological categories of the coming Messiah. In 11:23-26 Martha will also respond to Jesus' promise of eschatological newness with the conventional categories of her tradition (see page 88).

The Samaritan woman cannot comprehend the radical fullness of Jesus' words. She professes that when the Messiah comes, "he will show us all things," yet she stands talking with someone who has indeed "shown all things," and she does not know it. In verses 21-24 Jesus has shown the Samaritan woman a world in which new relations with God are possible, in which full relationship in spirit and truth is possible. Jesus has invited the woman to enter a world bounded neither by "this mountain" nor Jerusalem, a world determined by the inbreaking of the eschatological hour. Jesus has shown all this to the woman—and yet she still waits. She cannot let go of her traditional expectations enough to recognize the one with whom she speaks (cf. v. 10). What she "knows" about the coming Messiah (v. 25a) may actually prevent her from being fully open to the risk of the present experience of Jesus (cf. 3:2, 10).

Jesus' response to the Samaritan woman's traditional eschatological affirmations is simple and bold, "I AM, the one talking to you" (author's translation; v. 26). Translations of this verse downplay the boldness of Jesus' remarks by supplying a predicate for the *egō eimi* saying which is not present in the Greek. For example, the Revised Standard Version of this verse reads, "I who speak to you am he," and the New English Bible reads, "I am he, I who am speaking to you now." When the predicate is supplied, the meaning of Jesus' words becomes, "I am the Messiah you expect." The "I AM," however, cannot be taken simply as words of assent to Messianic identification. The "I AM" signifies that Jesus is the Messiah, but *more* than the Messiah. When Jesus speaks the "I AM" in verse 26, those words make explicit connections with the divine name of Exodus 13:14. Jesus speaks the "I AM" in its fullest sense here, to identify himself as the one who is sent from God (4:34), who is one with God (10:30).[18]

Jesus' words to the Samaritan woman in verse 26 are the final shattering of all her traditional categories. She accepted Jesus as a prophet (v. 19) and anticipated a future Messiah (v. 25). Jesus proclaims to her that the very one with whom she speaks is the one who is able to pronounce the "I AM," the one who is known through his relationship with God. Nothing in her tradition could have prepared her for the radical power of Jesus' self-revelation. No prior words in this text have had such an impact and force as the "I AM," nor have any other words been spoken so directly. In verses 10, 13-14, Jesus invited the woman to accept his offer of living water and new life, but the invitation was somewhat indirect, couched in irony, word play, and misunderstanding. At verse 26, all indirection is cast aside. The fullness of who Jesus is is revealed to the Samaritan woman. Will she now accept the offer of new life?

Transition: Return of the Disciples and the Departure of the Woman Verses 27-30

In these transitional verses, two events occur that effect the subsequent movement of the story. First, the disciples return from the city where they have gone to get food (v. 8). They arrive at the well while Jesus is still talking with the Samaritan woman. That Jesus would converse with a strange woman in public contradicts all the social conventions to which the disciples are accustomed, and their response is to marvel. We know from the Nicodemus story, however, that to marvel is precisely the wrong response to make to Jesus' unconventional words and deeds (cf. 3:8-10). To marvel is to show oneself closed to what Jesus has to offer. Perhaps the disciples are aware of this as well, because none of them gives voice to their amazement. They keep their disbelieving questions to themselves (v. 27). They will not risk making their amazement known to Jesus.

Second, the woman departs from the well and returns to her city. When she departs from the well, she leaves her water jar behind (v. 28). This minute narrative detail has intrigued commentators, who have imbued it with all levels of symbolic meaning. While some of the symbolism has heuristic value (e.g., the suggestion that leaving the water jar behind marks the end of one stage of the woman's life),[19] there is a tendency toward broad allegorization in the interpretation of this detail. It seems wiser to understand this detailed reference to the woman's jar as an indication that the story is not yet through with her. Much as verse 8 looked forward to the return of the disciples with food, verse 28 suggests the continued presence of the woman in the story.

What is most important about the woman's departure is not that she leaves her water jar, but what she does after she departs. She returns to the city and bears witness of Jesus to the townspeople: "Come, see a man who told me all that I ever did. Can this be the Christ?" (v. 29). The woman's words are both overstatement and understatement; overstatement because Jesus did not tell her *all* that she ever did—he only recounted her marital history; understatement because in verses 21-26 Jesus actually told her much more than *all she ever did*. The woman's "all that I ever did" stands in ironic juxtaposition to the words she spoke about the Messiah ("he will show us all things") in verse 25. The woman's question in verse 29, "This can't be the Christ, can it?" (author's translation), also stands in ironic juxtaposition to verses 25 and 26, especially to Jesus' bold "I AM" statement.

The woman is still bound by her traditional expectations of who and what the Messiah is. Her faith in Jesus is therefore inchoate and somewhat tentative, yet she is still moved by and open to the presence of Jesus enough to want to share the news of Jesus with others. In this act of sharing news, the woman does one very important thing that Nicodemus did not do—she bears witness to Jesus (cf. 1:11). Her categories of faith may still be tradition-bound, but she is not completely closed and she wants others to experience what she has experienced. The woman bears witness, and her townspeople come out to see Jesus (v. 30).[20] The movement of the Samaritan townspeople toward Jesus provides the frame (vs. 30, 39) for the conversation between Jesus and his disciples.

Jesus and His Disciples
Verses 31-38

The scene changes abruptly with the Samaritan woman's departure in verse 28. The narrative has focused exclusively on her encounter with Jesus, but now the focus shifts. The woman, who has been in the foreground, recedes to the background, and the disciples, who have been in the background, advance to the foreground. Verses 7-26 presented the encounter of an outsider with Jesus; verses 31-38 present the encounter of insiders with Jesus. As noted earlier, the one constant is Jesus.

The disciples were absent during the opening verses of John 4:4-42 because they had gone away to the city to get food (v. 8). That the first words they speak to Jesus upon their return (cf. the unspoken words of v. 27) are about food, therefore, does not surprise the reader. They say to Jesus, "Rabbi, eat" (v. 31). What is a surprise is Jesus' response: "I have food to eat of which you do not know" (v. 32). From whence has Jesus' food come (cf. v. 11), since the Samaritan woman has not even provided Jesus with a drink of water? The disciples are so puzzled that they say to one another, "Has anyone brought him food?" (v. 33). Notice that just as in verse 27, the disciples do not make their confusion known to Jesus, but attempt to keep it to themselves.

Jesus' response in verses 34-38, however, indicates that the disciples' confusion has not gone unnoticed. The Samaritan woman understood "living water" to refer to some form of miraculous drinking water, and therefore could not comprehend what Jesus was offering her. The disciples make a similar mistake here. When Jesus mentions food to eat, the disciples think he has gone ahead and eaten something while they were off in the city. This understanding, like the Samaritan woman's, falls short. In both cases, the misperception hinges on inadequate or misplaced knowledge. If the woman "*knew* the gift of God and who it is" that was speaking to her, she would ask for living water. Jesus has food of which the disciples "do not *know.*" In Jesus' conversation with the Samaritan woman, he and the woman moved slowly, as he invited her to accept his offer of new life. Only at the end of their engaging conversation does he boldly and directly supply the woman with what she needs to know.

By contrast, Jesus begins to explain things to his disciples in his opening words of verse 34: "My food is to do the will of him who sent me, and to accomplish his work." Any misunderstanding about the nature of the food about which Jesus speaks is now removed. Now the disciples are able to "know" about the food that sustains Jesus. The food that sustains Jesus is his vocation— to do God's will and to accomplish God's work. The Samaria narrative opened with the words "He had to pass through Samaria" (v. 4), and we located those words in the context of Jesus' vocation. Those words take on even more significance in the light of verse 34. The disciples think of food in terms of bread and fish that can be purchased in the city, much as the Samaritan woman thought of living water in terms of springs and water jars. Jesus, however, knows that his food, that which nourishes him, is to do God's will.

If the disciples can understand food and nourishment in terms of work and vocation, then they will be able to receive the offer of new life. For this to happen, however, the disciples' categories must also be shattered. Verses 35-38 function to move the disciples, and the reader, toward new categories. The shattering of the old and introduction of the new takes on a different form in verses 35-38. These verses are a series of agricultural proverbs that are loosely connected to one another. The metaphor of the harvest, and in particular of sowing and reaping, unites the various proverbs. The metaphor of food as vocation is expanded to include harvest as mission, as Jesus turns the focus from his own vocation to that of his disciples. That which sustains and feeds is to work for others. As Jesus' food was to complete the work of the one who sent him, the disciples' harvest is to complete the work begun by Jesus. The disciples' vocation is dependent on and derivative from God's work in Jesus (vs. 37-38). The disciples enter into the labor of others who have preceded them, and in that labor, new life is possible.

In verses 34-38, Jesus teaches his disciples through the medium of agricultural proverbs. The tone of this exchange with the disciples is quite different from that with the Samaritan woman. There is none of the playful give and take of verses 7-26, because in these verses Jesus resolves any misunderstandings as soon as they appear. In fact, there is no real dialogue in these verses, because the disciples' question in verse 33 is directed to themselves, not to Jesus. Jesus teaches with the prophetic voice of the one who does "the will of him who sent me," and the disciples, and the reader, are asked to listen and learn.

This section of metaphors of vocation and mission takes on particular significance when understood in its narrative context. While Jesus and the disciples are speaking, the Samaritans are coming toward Jesus, coming to see if he indeed could be the Christ. The Samaritan woman has born witness to Jesus' word and presence. The question that can now be asked in the context of these harvest teachings is, will her witness bear fruit? Will new life possibilities be available to all?

Jesus and the Samaritan Townspeople
Verses 39-42

In verse 30 the reader learned that the residents of Sychar were coming out to the well to see Jesus. In verse 39 the reader learns that the reason for their journey is more than idle curiosity: "Many Samaritans from that city believed in him because of the woman's testimony, 'He told me all that I ever did.'" For the first time in this chapter, we read of someone believing in Jesus. It is unclear what precisely the Samaritans believe, since their belief is dependent on the woman's tentative testimony (v. 29), but what is clear is that they are open to Jesus. As a result of their openness and belief, they invite Jesus to stay with them, "and he stayed there two days" (v. 40).

After Jesus' stay with the Samaritans, "many more believed because of his word" (v. 41). The woman's testimony led some to faith; Jesus' word brings more to faith. The Samaritan woman is cast in the unlikely role of the sower and laborer in the field (see vs. 38-39), because it is her work among the Samaritans that made them ripe for faith. It is a surprising and unlikely role, because the Samaritan woman herself never demonstrated full faith and knowledge. Even in her testimony of verse 29, she attempted to understand Jesus through her traditional categories of prophet and Messiah, rather than allowing her categories to be transformed by Jesus. The success of the woman's testimony in spite of herself demonstrates the power of the experience of Jesus, which will transform and transcend preconceived categories even in the face of ignorance, recalcitrance, and outright opposition. The discussions of John 9 and 11 which follow in our next chapters will further demonstrate the transforming power of Jesus even in the face of opposition.

By asking Jesus to come stay with them, the Samaritans make the request that the Samaritan woman herself could never quite make (vs. 10, 15), and offer the hospitality that the Samaritan woman had refused (v. 9). In the face of their belief in Jesus and the power of Jesus' own word, traditional constraints on Samaritan/Jewish relations become immaterial. Why? Because the Samaritans know "that this is indeed the Savior of the world" (v. 42). The Samaritans know who it is that is speaking to them (cf. vs. 10, 26).

The Samaritan woman had suggested that Jesus might be the Messiah for whom they were waiting. The Samaritans, when they hear Jesus for themselves, understand that Jesus cannot be labeled according to those traditional categories. Jesus is neither the Messiah the Samaritans expect, nor the Messiah the Jews expect. Jesus is the Savior of the world, and traditional expectations pale in the light of this confession.[21] The hour has indeed come when true worship will be defined neither by "this mountain" nor by Jerusalem. Jesus offers new life possibilities to all. The offer of new life is Jesus' food. The acceptance of that offer is our drink.

Conclusion

John 4:4-42 has taken the reader on a long journey, with many interruptions in the itinerary. The text has moved us from a Samaritan woman who balks at Jesus' request for water, to the disciples who are ignorant of Jesus' food, to the Samaritan townspeople who open their city and their lives to Jesus. The one constant in this journey has been Jesus, who invites the Samaritan woman to new life, who invites the disciples to new life and new vocation, and who stays with the Samaritan townspeople so that they might know new life. The text ends with a powerful confession: "This is indeed the Savior of the world," and we begin to see why Jesus "had to pass through Samaria."

When preaching this long and intricate text, it will be helpful to keep the closing words of the Samaritan townspeople in mind, "for we have heard for ourselves." It is the responsibility of the preacher to allow all members of the congregation to have that experience of "hearing for themselves." If the sermon on John 4:4-42 can be informed by the give-and-take between Jesus and the woman, the questions and misunderstanding, the boldness of Jesus, the tentativeness of the woman and the disciples, then the invitation to new life offered in the text will become an invitation for the congregation as well.[22] We must be careful not to present too readily the resolution of the story, either the "I AM" of verse 26 or the confession of verse 42, because if we abandon the rich textures of this text in favor of clear-cut announcements, Jesus' invitation will not be heard and who Jesus is will be lost.

It is urgent that our congregations are enabled to join the Samaritans in saying, "we have heard for ourselves," because

> How are they to believe in him of whom they have never heard? And how are they to hear without a preacher? And how can people preach unless they are sent? As it is written, "How beautiful are the feet of those who preach good news!" But they have not all obeyed the gospel; for Isaiah says, "Lord, who has believed what he has heard from us?" So faith comes from what is heard, and what is heard comes by the preaching of Christ (Romans 10:14b-17).

Jesus invites us all to move beyond a world bound by the traditions of Samaritans and Jews to a world where worship in spirit and truth is possible. It is in preaching that Jesus' invitation is made newly available. It is newly available "in this hour."

3

The Risk of Experience: How Do We Know and What Do We See? (John 9:1-41)

Our studies of John 3 and John 4 have demonstrated that if we approach and attempt to appropriate the Johannine Jesus through our own carefully circumscribed categories, we will miss the invitation to faith offered by the Fourth Gospel text. Nicodemus (3:1-15) is settled in his understanding of what qualifies a person as a teacher from God, what kind of deeds and words such a teacher can offer, and what the logical and permitted possibilities for the conduct of human life are. He is so settled that it is impossible for him to risk the act of faith that would transform his world. Nicodemus' world, in which he lives securely as "a ruler of the Jews," provides a comfortable and predictable womb for Nicodemus. He will not emerge from this womb to accept the offer to be born *anōthen*. Instead Nicodemus blusters in protest, his words an attempt to prevent the end of his comfortable, known world. Nicodemus is bound by the comfort of slogan.

The Samaritan woman (4:4-42) is neither so settled nor so comfortable as Nicodemus, and perhaps for that reason is more open to Jesus. Her personal history makes her somewhat of an oddity in her community, and as a Samaritan, she stands decidedly as an outsider in relation to Judaism. Yet, as we have seen, even this woman, with less to lose, is bound by circumscribed categories in her response to Jesus. If we understand Nicodemus as bound by *the comfort of slogan*, then the Samaritan woman is bound by *the comfort of tradition*. Her response to Jesus is

53

dictated by her understanding of the traditions of the patriarchs, of the relationship between Samaritans and Jews, of traditional Messianic expectations. The Samaritan woman is willing to engage in sustained dialogue with Jesus (which Nicodemus was unwilling to do), but her responses are so governed by her traditional understanding and expectations that she cannot grasp the radical redefinition of such traditions realized by the presence of Jesus. She hears and receives only that for which her tradition has prepared her, but cannot grasp that which moves beyond her traditional expectations.

Like Nicodemus and the Samaritan woman, we, too, are frequently guided by the *comfort of slogan* and the *comfort of tradition* when we approach the biblical texts and the claims they make upon us. The claims of these texts can be so radical that we must domesticate them, must filter them through less dangerous categories before we are willing to affirm them. The challenge to preachers and teachers of this word is to be faithful enough to the text to abandon such self-protective exercises and allow the word to confront us in its fullness. When our approach to biblical texts is to look for points or lessons which we can distill from them, we are more likely to evade such confrontations with the word, because such an approach means that we do not have to risk the full experience of the claim of the biblical texts.

The stories of John 3 and John 4 are not stories simply to be reported and commented on in preaching and teaching but are stories to be experienced, to move with, to be claimed by. In order to be confronted by the text in all its fullness, and to make that fullness available for those to whom we preach, we need to allow the texts themselves to shape our proclamation. The Lenten lectionary texts from the Fourth Gospel offer us a portrait of Jesus, but this Jesus may not be who we initially think he is or who we would like him to be. We must allow ourselves to be changed by the Jesus we encounter in these Johannine texts and allow our expectations and presuppositions about Jesus to be changed as well. A key to moving from the *comfort of slogan and tradition* to the *risk of experience* is to accept the narrative dynamics of these Johannine texts as part and parcel of the revealed encounter with Jesus. The subsequent challenge is to respect these dynamics when we retell these stories to others.

John 9:1-41 is a dramatic embodiment of the clash between

comfort and risk, between closed categories and open possibilities in the encounter with Jesus. The man born blind, in even more basic ways than the Samaritan woman, has nothing to lose in the encounter with Jesus and so is open to who Jesus is and what Jesus has to offer. The Pharisees, in contrast, have much to lose and therefore much to protect, and they, even more intensely than Nicodemus, fight to maintain their known world. In order to communicate the power and poignancy of this clash, this rich text must not be reduced to a series of propositions along the lines of: "The blind man stands for . . .," "The Pharisees stand for . . .," "The moral of the story is . . . ." John 9:1-41 is a long and intricate text, and only by staying with this story from beginning to end will we be able to speak of what it means to know and to see.

The Structure of John 9:1-41

John 9:1-41 is a carefully constructed story of interlacing narrative and dialogue that cannot be reduced to a simple plot line without destroying most of the effect of the story. The simple plot line, that a blind man is healed and subsequently cross-examined and rejected by the Pharisees, reflects neither the complicated dynamics of the gradual dawning of faith in the blind man nor the narrative interplay that leads the reader to reexamine his or her own preconceptions about knowledge and sight.

The dramatic structure of John 9 has been frequently noted.[1] The chapter is composed of seven tightly constructed scenes, which can be helpfully grouped together in three units:

I. Introduction: The Healing
Scene 1 (vs. 2-7)   Jesus heals the blind man
II. The Interrogations
Scene 2 (vs. 8-12)   Interrogation of the blind man by his neighbors
Scene 3 (vs. 13-17)   Interrogation of the blind man by the Pharisees
Scene 4 (vs. 18-23)   Interrogation of the blind man's parents by the Pharisees
Scene 5 (vs. 24-34)   Second interrogation of the blind man by the Pharisees

III. Conclusion: The Response
Scene 6 (vs. 35-38) Jesus and the blind man
Scene 7 (vs. 39-41) Jesus and the Pharisees

The reader is drawn from scene to scene as the story unfolds, and this movement increases the reader's participation in what is taking place in the narrative.

This schematic outline of the seven scenes of John 9 shows that Jesus is present at the beginning and end of the story, but is absent in the middle. Jesus is absent from verses 8-34, his longest absence from the narrative anywhere in the Fourth Gospel.[2] Jesus' words and deeds in verses 2-7 set the remainder of the story in motion, and verses 8-34 demonstrate the resistance and responsiveness that Jesus evokes. When Jesus reenters the story in verses 35-41, those who have resisted Jesus and those who have responded to Jesus are both called to accountability.

The narrative reality of Jesus' prolonged absence in John 9 is important to bear in mind as we move through the text. The focus of John 9 is on the *response* to Jesus, and Jesus does not need to be physically present for the broad spectrum of reactions to Jesus to be explored. Even though Jesus is physically absent, he remains the catalyst for all that takes place. Not one scene goes by in which the focus of attention is not in some way on Jesus. The real subject of the interrogations of verses 8-34 is Jesus, not the blind man.

As much as Jesus is talked about in the interrogations of verses 8-34, Jesus' name is never named after verse 11. In the blind man's first description of his healing, he identifies the healer as "the man called Jesus," but after that Jesus is only referred to as "he" (v. 15), "this one" (v. 16), or "that one" (v. 28).[3] There are many reasons for this reluctance to name Jesus' name. The Pharisees do not name the name of Jesus because to do so would give credence and standing to the one who bears the name. The man born blind does not name the name because the significance of the name will only dawn on him as the narrative advances. The man's parents do not name the name because they are afraid to do so (v. 23). Jesus is constantly the topic of conversation, but his name is not explicitly named!

The outline of John 9 thus presents us with one of the central paradoxes of this story: Jesus is physically absent as the story unfolds, but at the same time is rendered inescapably present through the words of the other characters who dialogue with one another. The absence of Jesus in much of this story gives it a peculiar contemporary relevance, because for the modern reader, Jesus is both absent and present.[4] Jesus is physically absent, but at the same time is rendered inescapably present through the words of the text. The next step is to render Jesus inescapably present through the words of the sermon, to communicate the power of Jesus' presence, even when he is absent.

The Text: The Healing
Verses 1-7

If Jesus is absent for most of John 9 and yet nonetheless functions as the dominant catalyst, then we may anticipate that those scenes in which Jesus is present and active will have particular importance in establishing the context out of which the rest of the story develops. As noted, Jesus is present when the story opens in verses 1-7, and it is to these introductory verses that we will first direct our attention.

The introductory scene of verses 1-7 can be broken into two parts: verses 1-5, which functions both as the introduction to the healing and as the prologue to the entire chapter; and verses 6-7, which constitutes the healing proper. Verse 1 opens with the observation that "he [Jesus] saw a man blind from his birth." The two main characters of the story, Jesus and the blind man, are thus introduced, but the two do not immediately enter into any kind of relationship. Instead, the scene is interrupted by what at first glance appears to be a diversion, as Jesus and his disciples engage in dialogue. The man born blind has no part in this opening conversation.

The conversation between Jesus and his disciples in verses 2-5 is the first example of a literary pattern that recurs throughout chapter 9, that of question and answer. Each dialogue in chapter 9 is structured around this pattern, and the relationship between the question asked and the answer given is particularly important to notice. The relationship between the two is not always what one would anticipate. In verse 2 the disciples ask, "Who sinned, this man or his parents, that he was born blind?" Jesus answers that neither sinned, but that the man was blind "that the works of God might be made manifest in him." Jesus' answer indicates that the disciples' question is not the right way to see what is before them. The disciples ask about the *cause* of the blindness; Jesus answers about the *purpose*. Such a disparity between question and answer will be frequent in John 9.

Jesus' answer to his disciples establishes the context in which the upcoming healing must be understood. If the blindness is understood only as a physical infirmity, visited upon someone who "deserves it," then what is really operative in the healing will be missed. The disciples' question reflects traditional categories of the relationship between suffering and sin. Jesus' answer indicates that these traditional categories are inadequate to comprehend the works of God. The blind man is indeed physically blind. He has been that way from birth, but more is at stake in this healing than the gift of sight. Just as the transformation of water into wine at Cana must be understood as a manifestation of glory that leads to belief (2:11), so too must the healing of the blind man be understood. It is an occasion for the manifestation of the presence and power of God that summons us to faith.

In addition to their function in establishing the proper context for interpreting the healing miracle, verses 1-5 also introduce many themes that will reappear, in a variety of forms, throughout the narrative. The themes of blindness, sin, the works of God, the contrast between day and night, and Jesus as the light of the world will be important motifs in the unfolding of the story. In many ways this prologue stands distinct from the rest of chapter 9 (for example, the disciples disappear after these verses), but in other more foundational ways, these opening verses cannot be separated from what follows. As our analysis of John 9 progresses, it will become increasingly clear how crucial the themes of verses 1-5 are to a full understanding of the chapter.

After these introductory verses, the story moves on to the actual healing. The narration of the healing stands in marked contrast to the eloquence of verses 1-5. Jesus' words in verses 3-5 are grand and serious, whereas his actions in verses 6-7 are more earthy, direct, and surprisingly understated. The two sections are explicitly connected by the narrator: "as he said this, he spat on the ground . . ." (a connection made even more explicit in the Greek text by the use of a participle), and this connection

heightens the contrast. Jesus speaks of doing the works of God—
and his next action is to spit on the ground! Jesus identifies
himself as the light of the world—and he makes clay out of the
spittle with which he then anoints the blind man's eyes! The
Fourth Evangelist does not draw the lines we tend to draw
between theological eloquence and material necessity.

One would expect the works of God to be manifested in a
loftier mode. One would expect the works of God to be manifested through the laying on of hands or the power of the spoken
word (cf. the healing of John 5:1-9), but instead Jesus practices
folk medicine. He anoints the man's eyes with mud and sends him
away to wash. A similar method of healing occurs in Mark 8:22-
26, where Jesus also uses spittle to restore sight to a blind man. In
Mark, the earthiness of the method of healing is accentuated
when Jesus has to try twice to restore sight to the blind man.[5]

The mode of healing in verses 6-7 may not be what one
would anticipate, but it is successful: "So he [the blind man] went
and washed and came back seeing." Taken out of their context,
verses 6-7 succinctly present the gift of sight to a man born blind.
Taken in the context of verses 1-5, they present the manifestation
of the works of God. Spittle and clay may not be where we would
expect to see God's presence lodged, but then we would also not
expect the Word to become flesh and dwell among us (1:14).

The blind man's posture during this healing is noteworthy. In
verse 1 the reader is told that Jesus notices the blind man, but
there is no indication that the blind man is aware that Jesus is
there. The blind man's presence is accentuated by the disciples'
question regarding him (v. 2), but Jesus' subsequent answer shifts
the focus away from the blind man to himself and God. With this
shift of focus, the blind man recedes out of narrative purview, so
that the initiation of the healing in verse 6, with no prior conversation between Jesus and the blind man, is a bit jarring. In contrast to most other gospel healing stories (cf. Mark 5:21-34;
7:24-30; 9:14-29), the blind man does not request the healing, nor
does he even speak. The blind man is acted upon and is not an
actor in his own healing.

The blind man voices neither *his need* nor *his faith* as a
motivation for Jesus to heal him. Nor does he acknowledge Jesus
as a healer. This posture provides a striking contrast to the healing of blind Bartimaeus in Mark 10:46-52. In that story, Barti-

maeus calls out to Jesus in faith, asking that his sight be restored
(Mark 10:48, 52). With Bartimaeus, faith precedes healing. With
the blind man of John 9, however, faith does not precede healing.
Rather, faith follows healing. The Bartimaeus story highlights
Bartimaeus' trusting faithfulness and Jesus' response to that faithfulness. Bartimaeus' faith is freely given because it precedes the
gift of sight. The Johannine story reverses that equation. Jesus'
healing of the blind man is unwarranted and unmotivated by
anything the blind man has done to demonstrate his "right" to
sight. The gift of sight is freely given because it precedes any
response of faith. The healing is an unencumbered act of grace.
Such graciousness may be what it means to speak of the manifestation of God's works (9:3).

   We have noticed the intricate interrelationship between Jesus'
presence and absence in John 9. Jesus is present in verses 1-7 up
until the point when he sends the man away to wash. But importantly, Jesus is not present when the blind man receives his sight.
The blind man "washed and came back seeing," but he does not
come back to Jesus. The blind man (now the formerly blind man)
and Jesus will not encounter one another again until verse 35.
Much will transpire between this first meeting of Jesus and the
blind man, out of which the man receives his sight, and their
second and final meeting. In the intervening verses, the focus will
be on the response to the healing and the healer. The gift of sight
to the blind man not only has an impact on the one who received
his sight, but also on all who learn of it and come into contact
with this blind man who can now see.

The Interrogations
Verses 8-12

   The first people that the man born blind comes into contact
with after he has received his sight are his neighbors and those
who had seen him before. The opening verse of this second scene
provides the reader with a new piece of information—the man
was not only blind, he was also a beggar. Like Bartimaeus in
Mark 10:46-52, the man's blindness has resulted in economic
deprivation and social marginality. His blindness has robbed him
of economic independence, of access to the goods of the social

system, and so he can only sit and beg.[6] His dependency is accentuated by the reference to his neighbors, as "those who had *seen* him before as a beggar." The man born blind had never seen anyone before.

This group of neighbors, when confronted by their neighborhood blind beggar who can now see, asks the man three questions. Their first question focuses on the identity of the man born blind: "Is not this the man who used to sit and beg?" This question, however, is not addressed directly to the man, but is asked among themselves. The group of neighbors feels the need to test the reliability of their own vision. The question about the man's identity draws a mixed response: "Some said, 'It is he'; others said, 'No, but he is like him'" (v. 9). This will not be the only time in John 9 that the blind man evokes a split reaction. The miracle that has occurred, the gift of sight to a man born blind, is so radical that those who are confronted by it try to find easy and logical ways to explain it away. The first attempt to explain the miracle away is to doubt the man's identity, to say that he is not the blind beggar but someone who resembles him. If it is a different man, then we can rest more easily, our sense of order and propriety preserved.

The man born blind puts an immediate end to all such speculation, however. With his first words of the chapter, he boldly announces his identity, "I am [the man]." It is probably more than a coincidence that the expression with which the man born blind announces who he is, "I am" (*egō eimi*), is the same expression used by Jesus throughout the Fourth Gospel to announce who he is (cf. 4:26). The reader of the Fourth Gospel has come to understand the *egō eimi* sayings as bold statements of identity, and the use of that bold and direct expression here signals that all equivocation about the man's identity will cease. He *is* the one whom they had seen before as a beggar.

Since they can no longer evade the miracle by disputing the man's identity, the neighbors' second question focuses on how the healing occurred: "Then *how* were your eyes opened?" (v. 10). The blind man answers this question by retelling the healing of verses 6-7. The man's recounting of the healing (v. 11) is almost as long as the original narration of the event. Such detail in the man's recounting indicates that even though he was a blind and silent partner during the healing, he was carefully attuned to what was being done to him. The blind man identifies Jesus by name, and as mentioned, this is the last time a character speaks Jesus' name in the chapter. The phrase with which the blind man speaks of Jesus, "the man called Jesus," is a distanced use of the name of Jesus, however, and reflects no ownership of the name. The identity of Jesus has no more significance to the man than any other detail of the healing.

The neighbors' third and final question focuses not on the man who has been healed, but on Jesus. They ask a question that could also be the reader's question at this point in the narrative: "Where is he?" Where is the man who you say has done this? Why is he not with you? Why are you not with him? Why is Jesus absent from the story now, just when we think he should stand up and be counted as the worker of miracles? "Where is he?"

The man's response is terse and to the point, "I do not know" (v. 12). In contrast to the Pharisees, who will figure prominently in the rest of the chapter, the man is quite willing to admit his ignorance. He has been asked a question to which he does not know the answer, and he is free enough to say so. The reader may marvel at his nonchalance with regard to Jesus (cf. John 5:13) or at his lack of thanksgiving (cf. Luke 17:11-19), but the Fourth Evangelist does not direct the story in those directions. Instead the evangelist presents the reader with a man who is naive, innocent, and guileless enough to say, "I do not know." The man stands in contrast with Nicodemus, who clung stubbornly to what he knew (cf. 3:9-10). As the rest of John 9 will indicate, the ability to admit that something lies outside of one's range of knowledge is a critical beginning point.

Verses 13-17

The neighbors, however, are not so guileless. They bring the man born blind to the Pharisees. The order of the neighbors' world has been disrupted—a blind man who used to sit on their streets and beg now sees and converses with them. They turn to those who sit in authority, so that those in authority can make sense out of the disorder and reassure them that how it "used to be" remains how it is and how it will be.

When the neighbors bring the man to the Pharisees, the narrator informs the reader that the healing occurred on the Sabbath (v. 14). Sabbath violation is not the center of controversy in this story, however. In John 5:1-18 the controversy over the Sabbath gives way to a more essential controversy over the relationship between Jesus and God (5:17-18). In similar fashion, the Sabbath controversy in John 9 provides a traditional context for the story, but is not the story's central thrust. Much more fundamental are questions of who this Jesus is who can heal and what response is called for in his presence.

The Pharisees continue the interrogation of the blind man. They ask him the same question the neighbors asked: How did you receive your sight? (v. 15). The man's answer is more abbreviated than his response to his neighbors, trimmed down to the essentials, "He put clay on my eyes, and I washed, and I see." Nothing more is offered than the minimum required to answer the Pharisees' question.

After the man has responded, the Pharisees ask questions among themselves (v. 16). As with the neighbors' self-questioning, there is a division in the group, with some saying one thing and some another. The questions asked by the neighbors and those asked by the Pharisees have different foci, however. The neighbors were divided over the blind man's identity; the Pharisees are divided over Jesus' identity and whether or not he is from God (cf. 3:2). The neighbors are ignorant about the healing and so question the blind man. The questions begin with the blind man, move to the healing, and finally to Jesus. The Pharisees are more pointed in their questioning. Their questions begin with the healing, but move almost immediately to Jesus. This shift is evident in their last question in this stage of the interrogation, "What do you say about him, since he has opened your eyes?" (v. 17). The preliminaries are over, the question that counts has now been asked.

The man's answer, like his answer to the neighbors' question, is terse and to the point, "He is a prophet" (v. 17; cf. 4:19). The man's innocence and openness are still evident, because he does not equivocate before the religious authorities and try to frame his answer in a way that will please them. He simply tells the truth, regardless of the consequences. The man born blind has moved from referring to Jesus very objectively as "the man called Jesus" to identifying him as a prophet. As we know from John 4, the recognition of Jesus as prophet is only a partial confession of Jesus' identity, but it is a confession that moves in the right direction.

The neighbors and the Pharisees have asked three questions concerning Jesus:
(1) *Where* is he? (v. 13)
(2) *How* did he do it? (vs. 10, 15)
(3) *Who* is he? (v. 17).
It is the last question, the question of who Jesus is, that will take on the most weight as the narrative progresses.

Verses 18-23

The Pharisees do not want to have to accept this miracle of sight. Too much is at stake if they do, so they attempt to discredit it. If the miracle is discredited, then the miracle worker can be ignored. The Pharisees' tack in their effort to discredit the miracle is not unlike that taken by the neighbors. The neighbors attempted to deny the miracle by denying that the man who stood before them seeing was the blind beggar they had known before. The Pharisees want to deny the miracle by denying that the man had ever been blind. The neighbors' incredulity led them to attempt to deny the miracle. The Pharisees' denial, however, has a deeper source. The language used to describe the Pharisees' attitude is particularly striking: "The Jews *did not believe* that he had been blind and had received his sight . . ." (italics added).[7] That the Fourth Evangelist uses the verb "believe" here is an indication of how much is at issue. If the Pharisees believe that the man was blind, they may be required to believe other things as well.

In an attempt to settle whether or not this man was ever actually blind, the Pharisees interrogate the man's parents. They ask the man's parents two questions:
1) Is this your son, who you say was born blind?
2) How then does he now see? (v. 19).
Notice that the very wording of the first question, "who you say was born blind," casts doubt on the veracity of that claim. When the Pharisees ask the parents how it is that their son now sees, it is the third time this question has been asked in the narrative (cf. vs. 10, 15). The repeated asking of this question demonstrates to what lengths one will go to deny what stands before one. The Pharisees have heard the answer to this question, but they refuse to accept it.

Curiously, the parents respond as if they had been asked three

questions instead of two. To the first question asked by the Pharisees, if the man was indeed their son, the parents respond in the
affirmative, "*We know* that this is our son and that he was born
blind" (v. 20, italics added). To the second question asked, the
parents have nothing to answer: "but how he now sees *we do not
know*" (v. 21). The Pharisees' two questions have now been answered, but the parents continue to speak: "*nor do we know* who
opened his eyes." Yet no one had asked the parents who had
opened their son's eyes! The parents' answer to an unvoiced question reveals precisely the Pharisees' subtext in conducting the
interrogation and their real agenda: They want to get at Jesus. The
Fourth Evangelist has deftly crafted the parents' response in order
to place the narrative focus on the central Christological issue.

Two aspects of the parents' third answer deserve comment.
First, this third answer contradicts the second answer they gave.
The parents initially said that they did not know how the blind
man received his sight, but then they go on to say that they do not
know *who* opened his eyes. They recognize that the identity of the
healer is an issue (or even that a healer was involved). This indicates that they know more about the healing than they are willing
to let on to the Pharisees. When we read in verse 22 about the
parents' fear of the Jews, verses 20-21 have already demonstrated
implicitly how that fear manifests itself in their behavior.[8]

Second, the parents' third answer is important because of its
use of the expression, "who opened his eyes." The reader, who
has witnessed the healing in verses 6-7, knows that the answer to
the question, "how were your eyes opened?" is always "Jesus."
Allusion to the opening of the man's eyes, therefore, functions as
code language to evoke Jesus' presence (vs. 17, 26, 30; cf. also vs.
10 and 14). It is not inappropriate to see the expression function-
ing in that way in verse 21. Jesus' name may not be named in this
story, but his powerful presence as the one who opens eyes lingers
and will not be denied its say.

The parents' final words to the Pharisees are ironic, given
what has immediately preceded this scene. They tell the Pharisees
to ask their son himself: "Ask him, he is of age, he will speak for
himself." The irony is, of course, that the Pharisees have already
asked the man and he has indeed spoken for himself, but the
Pharisees have refused to hear. The repetition of the words of
verse 21 in verse 23 underscores the irony of the Pharisees' pre-

dicament. They questioned the man's parents because they were dissatisfied with the outcome of their interview with the man born blind, but the interview with his parents has not resolved anything. And what is worse, it throws the Pharisees right back to where they started—questioning the man himself.

Verses 24-34

Verse 23 repeated the parents' urging to the Pharisees that they ask their son himself. In verse 24 they do just that, and their second interrogation of the man born blind begins. Verses 24-34 are the richest scene in John 9, as the position of the Pharisees over and against the man born blind (and Jesus) becomes clearer.

The second interview begins with two interesting statements by the Pharisees: "Give God the glory; we know that this man is a sinner" (v. 24, author's translation). The first statement works on two levels. To give God the glory is the required, appropriate response of gratitude.[9] Taken on a second level, however, these words spoken by the Pharisees to the man born blind are ironic, because the Pharisees themselves will not give glory to God in response to the healing. Their efforts to discredit the miracle and to deny the power of Jesus as healer indicate that they do not recognize the glory of God manifested in Jesus' act (cf. 2:11, 11:4). They want the blind man to give glory to the God they can comprehend in traditional categories, not to the God who shatters all categories.

The Pharisees' second statement in verse 24 begins with the words, "We know . . . ." In this final interview between the Pharisees and the man born blind, the verb "know" plays a pivotal role. Much of the dynamics of the interview are determined by who says they know and what they say they know, who says they do not know, and who in fact possesses knowledge. The verb "know" in verse 24 is the Greek verb *oida*, as it is throughout chapter 9 (vs. 12, 20, 21 twice, 24, 25 twice, 29 twice, 30, 31). There are two verbs of knowing in Greek, *ginoskō* and *oida*, and both occur more frequently in the Gospel of John that in any other book of the New Testament: *ginoskō*, fifty-seven times; *oida*, eighty-four times.[10] Given this frequency, it is striking that only the verb *oida* appears in chapter 9, never *ginoskō*. It is even more striking when one realizes that *oida* is actually derived from a

Greek root for seeing (*id-*). In chapter 9, the Fourth Evangelist is establishing an intimate connection between sight and knowledge. His use of the verb *oida*, which is semantically linked to verbs of seeing, is not unrelated to his use of words with an innate double meaning in John 3. Thus, by the very language that the Fourth Evangelist uses in chapter 9 to speak of knowledge, he signals the reader that there is a connection between knowledge and sight. What that connection is will be revealed as the narrative moves to its conclusion.

The Pharisees' first profession of knowledge in this scene, then, is that they *know* that "this man" (Jesus) is a sinner. This profession of knowledge is a restatement of verse 16. At verse 16, however, the question of whether or not Jesus is a sinner caused a schism among the Pharisees. The Pharisees are now more confident in what they "know" and there is no longer any schism. The Pharisees tighten their ranks and present a united front against the man born blind and Jesus. The lines are sharply drawn—the Pharisees on one side, Jesus and the man born blind on the other. Jesus is aligned not with those in power, but with those who speak truth to power.

The relationship between self-professed claims to knowledge (as that of the Pharisees in v. 24) and the actual possession of knowledge is crucial to understanding how the narrative of chapter 9 resolves itself. We note, therefore, that the man born blind responds to the Pharisees' confident "we know" with a statement of both what he knows and does not know: "Whether he is a sinner, *I do not know*; one thing *I know*, though I was blind, now I see."[11] The man born blind, unlike the Pharisees, is reluctant to make categorical judgments and is willing to say what he does not know. Also unlike the Pharisees, he is willing to accept the data of his experience and to judge accordingly. The data of his experience is that once he was blind, but now he sees. The man born blind will not fall into the trap of judging Jesus according to categories determined by the Pharisees. He will judge Jesus according to his gift of sight.

The man's response that he was once blind but now sees triggers another set of questions for the Pharisees: "What did he do to you? How did he open your eyes?" (v. 26). The Pharisees, of course, have asked the man these questions before (v. 15) and have asked his parents these questions (v. 19). They have also received answers to these questions (v. 15), but they do not accept or believe the answers they have been given. They do not want to see what is before them.

The man answers the Pharisees with a rebuke ("I have told you already and you would not listen") and two questions ("Why do you want to hear it again? Do you too want to become his disciples?" [v. 27]). His rebuke is exactly to the point and his questions are structured to force the Pharisees to show their hand. The cleverness of the man's response is remarkable. With masterful irony, his remarks turn the tables on the Pharisees, and for the first time in the narrative, the examinee becomes the examiner. The Pharisees do not want to become Jesus' disciples, but their control of the interrogation to this point in the narrative has enabled them to avoid having to come clean about what they do want. The questions that the man born blind asks cut through the Pharisees' controlled artifice.

The Pharisees are enraged by this turn of events, rage captured in the words "they reviled him." Their first words are intended to clarify their position over against the blind man: You are his disciple/we are disciples of Moses. A literal translation of their words would read, "You are a disciple of that man, but we are disciples of Moses." Notice that once again Jesus' name is not mentioned. He is only alluded to as "that man." The Pharisees' refusal to acknowledge Jesus' name is one way for them to uphold the contrast between being a disciple of *Moses* and being a disciple of someone who does not even merit having his name mentioned. True discipleship is in the name of Moses. Discipleship in any other name—or in no name—can only be illegitimate.

The Pharisees' remarks reveal more about themselves than they intend, however, and instead of further establishing their own authority, they ironically undercut it. The Pharisees are certain that the choice between being a disciple of Jesus and a disciple of Moses is one of either/or, and so they hold up their Mosaic discipleship over and against Jesus. From the perspective of the Fourth Gospel, however, this insistence is the Pharisees' self-indictment. Moses and Jesus do not stand in opposition to one another. Rather, Moses' words point to Jesus, and true faith in Moses should lead to faith in Jesus (5:45-47). The Pharisees' appeal to Mosaic discipleship as part of their opposition to Jesus, therefore, is an act of unfaithfulness to Moses and the torah, not faithfulness. The Pharisees' antagonism toward Jesus disinherits them from their Mosaic heritage. The reader of the Fourth Gospel knows that to be a true disciple of Moses, one must be a disciple of Jesus also.

The Pharisees' remarks in verse 29 continue in much the same vein. They attempt to secure their position and their authority by stating what they know and do not know, but they actually undercut themselves again. They intend the contrast they establish between Moses ("we know that God has spoken to Moses") and Jesus ("but as for this man, we do not know where he comes from") to discredit Jesus, but instead they reveal their own ignorance. They are quite correct in what they know about Moses, but not knowing Jesus' origin is a telling ignorance, more telling because the Pharisees have no real sense of what it is they do not know. One of the most important and ironically charged questions in the Fourth Gospel is where Jesus is from.[12] The essential identifying features of Jesus are that he is from above (e.g., 3:31; 6:38; 8:23), that he is from the Father (e.g., 3:34; 5:43; 6:46; 7:28-29; 8:42). The most basic misunderstandings in the Fourth Gospel are caused by not comprehending Jesus' origin (e.g., 1:11; 6:41-42; 7:27). The Pharisees' ignorance of Jesus' origin thus does not devalue Jesus. Rather, it shows their own distance from God. Their confident statement of what they know and do not know reveals how embedded they are in predetermined categories, so embedded that they cannot read the signs (v. 16) that are before them.

In verses 30-33 the man born blind responds to the Pharisees, and this speech is the longest by any character other than Jesus in this narrative. He confronts the Pharisees with the empirical evidence of his healing and its consequences, both of which they have been avoiding and denying. In these verses the man born blind takes over the Pharisees' categories of knowledge and skillfully uses them to indict the Pharisees. The man's response focuses on the Pharisees' acknowledgement that they do not know where Jesus is from. He opens with the bold statement that mocks the Pharisees, "Why, this is a marvel! You do not know where he comes from, and yet he opened my eyes." He then proceeds to demonstrate why indeed their ignorance is a marvel.

The man confronts the Pharisees with two pieces of data. First, he cleverly beats the Pharisees at their own game. The Pharisees have determined that Jesus is a sinner (v. 24), and yet, as the man born blind reminds them, "We know that God does not listen to sinners, but if any one is a worshiper of God and does God's will, God listens to him" (v. 31). Notice that the "we know" that the man born blind speaks is an inclusive "we," one that draws on the common heritage shared by the man and the Pharisees (see, e.g., Isaiah 1:15; Psalms 66:18; 145:19; Proverbs 15:8, 29; cf. John 9:16). The Pharisees have confidently asserted that "we know" (vs. 24, 29), but in this verse the man born blind tells them that if they really gave heed to what they know by virtue of who they are as Jews, they would be able to interpret correctly what is before them. The Pharisees have defended themselves against Jesus by appealing to their heritage. The man born blind turns that appeal to heritage so that it points toward Jesus instead of away from him.

Second, the man confronts the Pharisees with the incomparability of the act of healing (v. 32). The eyes of a man born blind have been opened, and "If this man were not from God, he could do nothing" (v. 33). Some of the Pharisees themselves had acknowledged this, but such a truth was too much for them to bear (v. 16). Instead they wanted to deny the very act of healing itself (v. 18), but the man born blind will not allow them to take that way out. He confronts the Pharisees with the truth that is right before their unseeing eyes. The data indicates that Jesus is from God, but the Pharisees refuse to see.

The Pharisees' response to the man brings chapter 9 full circle. In 9:2, Jesus' disciples inquired whether the man's blindness was a result of his sin. In our discussion of 9:2-3, we noted that Jesus' answer to the disciples' question indicates that the disciples are operating out of the wrong categories. If they understood the man's blindness to be a result of sin, they will be unable to see the manifestation of God's works in the healing. Now, in 9:34, the Pharisees are doing the very thing that Jesus urged against: "You were born in utter sin, and would you teach us?" The Pharisees' final words to the man born blind label him a sinner. They do not see God at work in the miraculous gift of sight. They see only an inveterate sinner. Like Nicodemus in John 3, the Pharisees did not believe the "earthly things" and are therefore blind to the "heavenly things" (cf. 3:11). They do not see God at work in the healing of the blind man, because God's healing works against all their preconceived categories.

The Pharisees also mock the ability of the man born blind to teach them. How can someone who is a born sinner attempt to teach them, the established religious authorities? The notion that they would be taught by a sinner is incongruous to them, yet in that incongruity lies the truth. The man born blind does teach them (the very length of his speech is evidence of that), but the Pharisees refuse to be taught. Despite their assumptions and assertions to the contrary, the Pharisees' official status as teachers has not provided them with access to the truth. The witness of the man born blind provides access to the truth, but the Pharisees will not listen. The Pharisees are so certain that they *know*, are so heavily invested in their own categories and definitions, that they cannot be open to what is taking place before them. The man born blind *would* teach them, but they are closed to his teaching. The Pharisees' final action is therefore sharp and decisive. What the man's parents had feared for themselves (v. 22) comes true for their son: "And they cast him out" (v. 34).

The Response to Jesus

The interrogations of verses 8-34 were all conducted in Jesus' absence. The focus of these verses is therefore the variety of responses that Jesus evokes. All the characters, but in particular the man born blind and the Pharisees, have grappled with the significance of the gift of sight that the man received and the identity of the one who bestowed that gift. In verses 8-34 Jesus is only indirectly present through the controversy that his act of healing occasions. In the concluding verses of chapter 9 (vs. 35-41), Jesus reenters the narrative, and both the man born blind and the Pharisees will have a direct encounter with Jesus. Jesus will call the man and the Pharisees to accountability for the stances they have taken with regard to him.

Verses 35-38

At verse 35, the man born blind once again finds himself on the outside. At the beginning of chapter 9 he was on the outside because he was blind and a beggar. Now he is on the outside because the Jewish authorities have cast him out. When he was a blind beggar, Jesus found him and gave him sight. Now, when he is a refugee from home and synagogue, Jesus finds him again. The initiative in their relationship still resides with Jesus.

Jesus' first words to the man born blind are, "Do you believe in the Son of man?" Every character who has approached the man in verses 8-34 questions him, and now Jesus does the same. The questions and answers of verses 35-38 are different from all that has preceded, however, because Jesus and the man born blind engage in genuine conversation. Jesus' question is not an act of intimidating interrogation, but offers him an invitation to faith. The man's readiness to believe is apparent in his question of verse 36, as he asks for a more precise identification of the Son of man so that he may indeed believe. The way in which Jesus responds to him is important: "You have seen him, and it is he who speaks to you" (v. 37). As with the Samaritan woman (4:10, 26), Jesus identifies himself in terms particular to his relationship with the man born blind, through reference to the man's gift of sight and to the conversation in which they are engaged. When the man hears these words of Jesus and understands that Jesus is the Son of man, his response is immediate and unequivocal, "Lord, I believe" (v. 38).

The openness to faith of the man born blind contrasts sharply with the closed, defended position of the Pharisees. Unlike the Pharisees, who would not believe what they had seen (v. 18), the man does believe what he sees. The man is not locked into his own categories, but allows his experience of Jesus to transform his categories from "the man called Jesus" to "Lord, I believe." The Pharisees looked at Jesus and the man born blind and saw sin. The man born blind saw the power and presence of God in his gift of sight and recognized Jesus as the one who made that power and presence available.

The last act of the man born blind in this narrative is to worship Jesus. The man recognized the transformative power of the gift of sight he received from Jesus and risked allowing that power to transform his life. (Cf. the healing of the lame man in John 5, where no similar redefinition of life takes place on the part of the one who is healed. Instead the healed man reports Jesus to the Jewish authorities.) The Pharisees branded the man born blind a sinner and cast him out, but Jesus found him and welcomed him home (cf. 10:3-4).

Verses 39-41

Verse 39 is the hermeneutical key to interpreting the entire chapter, but it receives its full significance for the reader only because the reader has experienced the contrast between the Pharisees and the man born blind throughout the telling of the story. The whole narrative of chapter 9 has been about sight and blindness, but as verse 39 makes clear, sight and blindness operate on many different levels. Throughout chapter 9, the central identifying feature of the man is that he is "the man born blind." From this we know that one way to be blind is to be *born* blind. In verse 39, however, Jesus speaks about another form of blindness that stands in contrast to being born blind. That form of blindness is to *become* blind: "Jesus said, 'For judgment I came into this world, that those who do not see may see, and those who see may become blind.'" Because of Jesus' presence in the world, those who are born blind may become sighted and those who are born sighted may become blind.

John 9:1-38 has demonstrated how and why such a transformation occurs, and verses 40-41 reenact that transformation in encapsulated form. Some of the Pharisees overhear Jesus speaking, and they ask, "We aren't blind, are we?" (author's translation; v. 40). The Pharisees still assert their sight and their knowledge, even after the narrative has conclusively demonstrated their blindness. They expect Jesus to answer, "No, you aren't blind" (the use of the interrogative particle *mē* in the Greek text indicates that they anticipate this response), but Jesus says just the opposite. Instead of affirming their sight, he indicts their blindness.

Jesus' final words in verse 41 show how much standard categories have been transformed by his presence. His words break into two parts. In verse 41a he says, "If you were blind, you would have no sin" (author's translation). This remark brings the reader back to verses 2-3. Chapter 9 opened with the disciples trying to find a connection between the man's blindness and sin. In verse 41 Jesus gives the final answer to their question—physical blindness is not a result of sin. The man born blind fits Jesus' words in verse 41a—one who is blind, but without sin, despite the Pharisees' assertions to the contrary. The innocence of the man born blind is confirmed by his willingness to say, "Lord, I believe."

In verse 41b Jesus turns from the blind man to the Pharisees: ". . . but now that you say, 'we see,' your sin remains" (author's translation). Since you assert your sight, even when you have none, your sin remains. Throughout the narrative the Pharisees have confidently asserted what they know, even when their "knowledge" conflicts with what they see, and now Jesus turns their words against them. Their indictment of the blind man in verse 34 was that he was born in utter sin, but that becomes their own indictment now. Because they are so sure that they know what counts for knowledge and truth, because they are so sure they have a corner on knowledge, the Pharisees cannot recognize truth when it stands before them. They, not the blind man, are the ones who sin, because they are not open to the truth, and indeed actively work to hinder its power and presence (cf. 8:21-24, 42-47). The Pharisees are so sure that they know what there is to know and how one is to know it, that they cannot be taught (vs. 27, 34). They are so sure that the categories according to which they understand life are the only viable and possible categories, that they cannot see the radical works of God made manifest in the healing of the blind man. The Pharisees are unwilling to risk opening up the categories through which they order life, and as a result, despite their protestations to the contrary, they cannot see and cannot know.

Conclusion

John 9 brings the reader face to face with the central questions of how do we see and what do we know. The answer the text offers is that we will never see and never know unless we risk the experience of Jesus. Our preconceived categories, our well-defended territory, may bring us comfort and security, but they will not lead to knowledge and sight, to healing and life. Unless we are willing to allow the experience of Jesus made available in this text to redefine who we are and what categories and labels we use, we will end up like the Pharisees—blind and alienated from the one source of life.

The challenge in preaching John 9 is to offer the experience of Jesus embodied in this text to those to whom we preach. The task of preaching this text is not merely to enable the congregation to *understand* what the story is *about*. The task of preaching is more specifically to enable the congregation to *experience* what this text *does*. As our exegesis of John 9 has demonstrated, this chapter is not a static presentation, but is a story built on intricate dynamics and interrelationships. When we enable our hearers to enter into those rich dynamics, we are faithfully preaching this text.

The task of preaching John 9, therefore, is not an easy one, given the length and narrative complexity of this chapter. Yet the very things which make preaching John 9 a challenge also make it richly promising. If we allow the mode in which John 9 speaks, with its finely drawn characters, its precisely demarcated scenes, and its animated dialogues, to inform our mode of preaching this text, then our sermon will do for the congregation what this text does for its readers. It will make present, through the power of the word, the Jesus who gives sight to the blind and who evokes decision and transformation.

4

From the Risk of Experience to the Gift of Life (John 11:1-53)

In our study of John 9, we noted the narrative's intricate interweaving of question and answer, denial and confession. As we moved through the story, we discovered that the key to being willing to risk the experience of Jesus lies in redefining how and what we know and see. Blindness and sight are found in many forms. The antithesis between the man born blind and the Pharisees derives in large measure from where each lodged their trust and how much each was willing to be transformed. The blind man was willing to be transformed by Jesus, and his transformation resulted in sight and healing. The Pharisees were unwilling to be transformed by Jesus, and their resistance resulted in blindness and sin.

The story of Lazarus in John 11 is the most radical narrative embodiment in the Fourth Gospel of one's willingness to be transformed and of Jesus' ability to transform. Yet as radical and singular an event as the raising of Lazarus is, this story is of a piece with the three other Johannine texts we have discussed. The relationship among these four texts has important implications for how we preach these stories during the Sundays of Lent. The order in which the four texts appear in the Lenten lectionary for Year A calls us to take seriously in our preaching the dynamic interrelationship of the four stories, in addition to the narrative integrity of each individual text. This sequence of Fourth Gospel texts on the second, third, fourth, and fifth Sundays of Lent provides a rich opportunity to move toward Easter with a full picture before us of the transformative power and presence of Jesus.

The chapter titles of this book have been chosen in order to indicate the interconnection of the four Johannine texts. The proposed movement that the titles suggest is from the comfort of *slogan* (John 3) and *tradition* (John 4) to the *risk of experience* (John 9) to the *gift of life* (John 11). For Nicodemus (John 3), the Pharisees (John 9), and to some extent the Samaritan woman (John 4), the operating assumption is that controlled slogans and traditional categories define and give life. But the truth is that life lies at the opposite end of the spectrum from each such controlled and controlling assumption. Life is only possible when its source is the one who gives life, Jesus. This means that life lies neither in traditional categories and definitions nor in the controlled safety of the reliable. Rather, life lies in exploding all such categories to reveal what really counts and has power. In many ways, the John 9 text is a transitional text between John 3 and 4 and John 11, because that text makes "visible" both approaches to life—that which clings to the known and reliable and that which is open to transformation. As we arrive at the story of John 11, we have seen both responsiveness to Jesus and resistance to Jesus, and have experienced glimpses of the radical newness that Jesus offers. In the story of the raising of Lazarus, the text for the last Sunday prior to Passion Week, the gift of life that Jesus offers is now fully visible, in all its grace and glory (11:4).

The Structure and Context of John 11:1-53

John 11:1-53 is the longest sustained narrative outside of the Passion account in the Fourth Gospel. It begins with the announcement that Lazarus is ill (11:1) and ends with the decision to put Jesus to death (11:53). The somber tone of these framing verses, with their movement from the illness of the one whom Jesus loves to Jesus' own death, is an important indicator of what is at issue in this narrative. The opening and closing verses indicate that the story that is told within this frame is more than just a healing story. It is a story that will somehow bring the reader closer to Jesus' impending death.

The plot of the story is rather straightforward: Jesus hears of Lazarus' illness, Jesus proceeds to the tomb, Jesus raises Lazarus, the authorities are distressed. Once again, however, as with the other texts we have studied, such a simple summary of the story does not begin to approximate the richness of the text before us. The plot line of John 11:1-53 does not indicate where this story places its emphasis, where it lingers, where it moves on without a backward glance. As our analysis of John 11 will show, the text does not always linger where the reader thinks it should linger, nor does it move on when the reader thinks it should move on. When preaching this long text, then, it is important not to rush immediately to what we think the story is "about," but instead to allow our movement through this text to be governed by the way in which the story itself unfolds.

John 11:1-53 can be divided into three basic parts: a prologue (1-16), the story proper (17-44), and an epilogue (45-53). Of these three units, the central unit, the story proper, can be further subdivided. One suggested outline for the structure of John 11:1-53 is the following:

I. Prologue	11:1-16
II. The Story	11:17-44
A. On the Way to the Tomb	11:17-37
1. Jesus and Martha	11:17-27
2. Jesus and Mary	11:28-37
B. The Tomb	11:38-44
III. Epilogue: The Aftermath	11:45-53

Several exegetical observations can be made on the basis of this outline. First, John 11:1-53 shares an important characteristic with John 9: The action of both stories is preceded by a prologue. In the discussion of John 9, we saw that the prologue (9:1-5) was critical for introducing the theological categories that informed the rest of the narrative and for establishing the interpretive lens through which the subsequent verses were to be read. We should be alerted, therefore, to read the prologue in John 11:1-16 with care.

Second, this structural overview of the material indicates that Jesus does not arrive at Lazarus' tomb until verse 38, and that the scene at the tomb lasts for only seven brief verses, a very small percentage of the fifty-three verses that constitute this story. Our tendency is to identify this story as the raising of Lazarus. While the raising is the singular decisive event of John 11:1-53, the way in which the story is told suggests that other aspects of the story deserve at least as much of our attention.

Third, and this observation is related to the preceding one, the outline indicates that the recounting of this miracle breaks with the usual Johannine pattern. In John 5, 6, and 9, the miracle (5:1-9; 6:1-14; 9:6-7) precedes the dialogue (5:11-19; 6:25-40; 9:8-41). In John 11, however, this relationship is reversed, as the heart of the dialogue (11:1-42) precedes the miracle (11:43-44). This, too, should be kept in mind as we read through this story.

Before proceeding to the detailed analysis of this text, a word about its context in the Fourth Gospel is called for, since that context has implications for how this text is preached. As alluded to earlier, this long passage ends with the words, "So from that day on they took counsel how to put him to death." The Lazarus story is the final catalyst that moves the Jewish authorities to act against Jesus. The Fourth Evangelist has quite explicitly positioned the Lazarus story in order to bring his readers to the death of Jesus.

The connection between the raising of Lazarus and the death of Jesus is unique to the Fourth Gospel. First, no other evangelist recounts this episode, and second, Matthew, Mark, and Luke all locate the decisive impetus for Jesus' death within the events of Jesus' final week in Jerusalem (e.g., Matthew 26:1-3; Mark 11:15-19). Critical scholarship continues to debate the relationship between the Lazarus story and the Synoptic Gospels and between the different traditions of the cause of Jesus' death.[1] Those questions will never be ultimately resolved. What matters for our purposes is that the Fourth Evangelist, in striking contrast to the other traditions about Jesus' death, structures the raising of Lazarus as the last act of Jesus' ministry before his Passion. The story of Lazarus is a radical demonstration of God's power for life (Romans 4:17) as manifested in Jesus, yet it is lodged in a context of death. With this context in mind, we now proceed to a detailed expository analysis.

The Prologue
Verses 1-16

The opening verses of chapter 11 introduce the reader to the members of a family whom Jesus loves (11:3, 5). The three family members involved are Lazarus and his two sisters, Mary and Martha. Lazarus is mentioned first, and just as chapter 9 opens

with a reference to the man blind from birth, chapter 11 opens
with a reference to Lazarus' illness (11:1—"a certain man was ill,
Lazarus of Bethany"). After Lazarus is named, his two sisters are
named (11:1, 2), and the family portrait then closes with another
reference to Lazarus and his illness.

The Fourth Evangelist thus uses a chiasmus to introduce this
family to the reader:

   ill Lazarus———►Mary-Martha-Mary◄———ill Lazarus.

The chiastic structure of these opening verses reflects the role the
three family members will play throughout the narrative. The
story is occasioned by Lazarus' illness and reaches its climax in
the raising of Lazarus. Between these two pivotal framing events,
however, Mary and Martha, in conversation with Jesus, occupy
the center of the story.

The Fourth Evangelist's identification of Mary in verse 2
deserves special attention. Mary is identified as the one who
anointed Jesus and wiped his feet with her hair. Mary's anointing
of Jesus is part of the Fourth Gospel narrative, but it does not
occur until chapter 12, *after* the Lazarus story. The Fourth Evangelist therefore anticipates himself when he describes Mary with
reference to the anointing in chapter 11. Is this proleptic identification a mistake, a slip on the narrator's part, or does it serve
some narrative and theological function? First, on a tradition-
critical level, this proleptic identification of Mary suggests that
the Fourth Evangelist is attempting to orient the reader to who
Mary is, i.e., which Mary, by identifying her on the basis of the
way she is known in the tradition, regardless of where the anointing is narrated in his gospel. We find a similar proleptic use of
traditional material in chapter 1. In 1:40 Andrew is identified as
Simon Peter's brother, although Peter is not introduced into the
narrative until 1:41.

The proleptic identification of Mary also has a more important theological function in this narrative, however. The anointing
of Jesus in chapter 12 is explicitly cast as a foreshadowing of the
preparation of Jesus' body for burial (cf. 12:3, 8; 19:39-40), an
anticipation of the Passion. By reminding the reader of Mary's
role in the anointing, the Fourth Evangelist draws the Passion
story into the story of Lazarus. The connection between the
Lazarus story and Jesus' death is therefore intentionally suggested by the Fourth Evangelist from the outset of chapter 11.

John 11 proceeds under the shadow of Jesus' death. The first action of the story occurs when the two sisters send a message to Jesus, informing him that Lazarus is ill (v. 3). Three aspects of this message are striking. First, for the third time in these opening verses, the reader hears that Lazarus is ill. The repeated reference to his illness suggests that the narrator wishes to draw attention to Lazarus' condition. Second, Lazarus is identified as the one whom Jesus loved. Prior to this point in the narrative, Jesus has healed strangers. Now he is confronted with someone in need whom he loves. Finally, the two sisters request nothing specific from Jesus. They merely inform him that Lazarus is ill. Their words are similar to the words that Jesus' mother speaks to him at the wedding in Cana. In that text, Jesus' mother informs him that there is no wine (2:3), but makes no explicit demand of Jesus. In both instances, however, the reader senses that even though the women ask nothing of Jesus, they address him because they expect him to know what to do.

Jesus' response to his mother in 2:4 is, "O woman, what have you to do with me? My hour has not yet come." Jesus was able to read his mother's unvoiced request and rebuffs her, because his actions will not be dictated, even by his mother. Jesus' response to the two sisters also indicates that their perception of the situation and their expectation of what Jesus should do are misguided. Just as 9:3-5 was critical for establishing the interpretive lens through which to see the healing of chapter 9, so too Jesus' response in 11:4 interprets in advance the events of the Lazarus narrative.

Jesus' response opens with the fourth reference to Lazarus' illness: "This illness is not unto death; it is for the glory of God, so that the Son of God may be glorified by means of it." When Jesus speaks of Lazarus' illness here, he announces the purpose and function of that illness. First, the illness is not unto death. These words simultaneously underscore the severity of Lazarus' illness and anticipate the life-giving miracle with which the story will close. Second, the illness is for the glory of God. The reader of the Fourth Gospel has already experienced a connection between the working of miracles and God's glory (2:11; 9:3), and 11:4 enables the reader to place the raising of Lazarus in that broader context of the manifestation of God in the works of Jesus.

The conclusion of 11:4 deserves special attention. Jesus connects Lazarus' illness and the manifestation of God's glory with the glorification of the Son of God. In 13:31 Jesus will explicitly link the hour of his Passion and the hour of his glorification, and he anticipates that connection here (cf. also 12:27-32). The allusion to the anointing in 11:2 hinted at a connection between the Lazarus story and Jesus' Passion; 11:4 makes that connection unavoidable. Lazarus' illness will not result in Lazarus' death, but it will instead result in Jesus' death and glorification. The beginning to this story causes us to hold in check any exclusively triumphalist reading we might be tempted to give this text, because it reminds us that there is no glorification apart from Jesus' death.

At the end of verse 4, then, the characters have been introduced and the scene set. The reader anticipates some action, some gesture on Jesus' part in response to the sisters' message. The reader is therefore not prepared for what follows—nothing!

Verse 5 reads, "Jesus loved Martha and her sister and Lazarus." Logic would dictate that Jesus would go to help those whom he loves, yet Jesus stays away longer (v. 6). The juxtaposition of verses 5 and 6 is jarring. The "so" with which verse 6 begins indicates a definite connection between Jesus' staying where he is and the love of verse 5, but it is not the kind of connection the reader has anticipated. Jesus' actions contradict the conventional dictates of logic, as they have throughout the Fourth Gospel. He told his mother that the wine supply was none of his concern, but then he transformed water into wine anyway (2:3-8). His brothers insisted that he go up to Jerusalem for the feast of Tabernacles. Jesus refused them, but then he went up anyway (7:1-10). Jesus cannot be controlled even by those closest to him, by his family and friends whom he loves. Jesus will deal with Lazarus, but that he stays away two days longer indicates that Jesus' actions will come on his terms and no one else's. At this juncture in the narrative, it is Jesus alone who understands that Lazarus' illness is for the glory of God. His actions must be understood as proceeding from that awareness.

When Jesus deems it to be the opportune moment ("then after this"), he initiates the movement toward Lazarus (v. 7). Jesus' words to his disciples, "Let us go into Judea again," indicate that his decision to go to Judea is as intentional as his decision to stay away was. Once again, Jesus determines when it is time to act. This verse is the first indication that the disciples are accompanying Jesus. Prior to this verse, the focus has been exclusively on Jesus and the family from Bethany.

Judea is not a place where Jesus is well loved and received. Jesus and his disciples are outside of Judea (10:40) because the Jews in Jerusalem have tried to stone him (10:31), yet Jesus now wants to return there. His disciples remind him of the Jews' attempt to kill him and question why he would willingly place himself again within their reach. The disciples' question, *"are you going* there *again?"* is a restatement of Jesus' initial command, *"Let us go* into Judea *again* (italics added)." The disciples' question explicitly reminds the reader that this story takes place under the shadow of Jesus' death.

Jesus answers his disciples with a metaphor about day and night. His reference to the number of hours in the day indicates that he is not hesitant about meeting his death, but goes readily to face the Passion because it is time for him to be about his business. Verses 9-10 consist of two parallel sentences, the first positive in meaning (walks in the day, does not stumble); the second negative (walks in the night, does stumble). The link between the two verses is the light metaphor. This metaphor works on two levels. The day and night imagery suggests initially that "the light of this world" refers to the sun, that light that distinguishes day from night and provides the light by which one can work. With this reading, Jesus' words emphasize the importance of taking advantage of the light that the sun makes available.

The light metaphor has a broader range of possibilities for the reader of the Fourth Gospel, however. In the Gospel prologue, the Fourth Evangelist uses the images of light and darkness to describe the conflicted relationship between Jesus and the world (1:5, 10). Throughout the Gospel narrative, light and darkness are used to represent the consequences of one's acceptance or rejection of Jesus (cf. 3:19-21). As noted in chapter 1, Nicodemus came to Jesus "by night" (3:2). The light imagery reaches a climax in 8:12 and 9:5, when Jesus identifies himself as the light of the world. The reader of the Fourth Gospel brings all of these associations to 11:9-10, and is therefore able to discern that Jesus speaks about more than merely the sun here. He speaks about himself and the ways in which his presence and the acceptance of his presence ("the light is not in him") are the ultimate criteria in distinguishing day from night (cf. 12:35-36).

There are important similarities between Jesus' words to his disciples that introduce the healing of the blind man (9:3-5) and his introductory words to his disciples here. In both stories Jesus raises the question of light and darkness, of acceptance and rejection. In both Jesus answers a quite specific question about one particular event with words that set what is to come in an explicit theological context. Both miracles are events that reveal God and God's dealings with the world.

After establishing the theological context for what is about to take place, Jesus returns to the subject of Lazarus. Up to this point in the narrative, Jesus and the reader know that Lazarus is ill, but the disciples do not possess that knowledge. When Jesus does tell his disciples about Lazarus, however, he does not use the word that has consistently characterized Lazarus in this story—"ill." Instead Jesus says that Lazarus sleeps, *koimaō*. Like the words *anōthen* ("from above"/"anew"), *pneuma* ("wind"/"spirit"), and *hupsoō* ("exalt"/"lift up") in John 3 that have two meanings, *koimaō* also is a word with a double meaning. It may mean sleep, or it may double as a euphemism for death. Both of these meanings are operative in this verse and in the disciples' subsequent misunderstanding. To the reader and Jesus, who know that Lazarus is ill, this verb suggests that Lazarus has died as a result of his illness. To the disciples, however, who are ignorant of Lazarus' condition, it suggests simply that Lazarus sleeps.

It is not surprising, then, that his disciples misunderstand Jesus (v. 12). Like Nicodemus and the Samaritan woman, they can only grasp the literal level of what Jesus says. Their response, which clearly does not understand sleep as referring to death, contains its own inadvertent ironic play on words. Its full meaning can be grasped by the reader but not by the disciples themselves. The disciples do not understand why Jesus would risk death in Judea simply because Lazarus sleeps, because if "he has fallen asleep, he will recover." The verb "recover" is the future passive of the Greek verb *sodzō*, "to save." In relation to disease, the passive of *sodzō* means "be restored to health," "get well," but other connotations of the verb cannot be categorically excluded.[2] In many of the healing stories of the Gospels, the sense of *sodzō* as "save," "deliver," frequently overlays its meaning as "get well" (cf. Mark 5:28, 34; 10:52), and a comparable dynamic is operative in this verse. That Lazarus will recover, i.e., that Lazarus will be restored or saved, means more in the context of this story than the disciples intend.

The narrator interrupts the story in verse 13 to make explicit what the reader already knows—Jesus and the disciples are conducting their conversation on two different levels. After the narrator speaks to the reader, Jesus speaks to his disciples: "Then Jesus told them plainly, 'Lazarus is dead.'" Unlike John 4, where Jesus allows the woman to linger in her misunderstanding, here Jesus resolves the misunderstanding almost as soon as it arises by stating quite clearly and boldly that Lazarus is dead. The reader and the disciples are now back on even footing, and Jesus alone understands the real significance of Lazarus' death: that it is for the glory of God (11:4).

Jesus' words in verse 15 provide an explanation for his actions of verse 6: "and for your sake I am glad that I was not there, so that you may believe." Jesus did not stay away from Lazarus because he was indifferent, but so that the disciples might believe. Verse 15 connects with verse 4, and brings the glory of God back into focus (cf. 2:11, where the manifestation of glory in a sign is also the occasion for the disciples to believe). Jesus will return to Judea and risk death for the sake of his disciples and their faith. Jesus' last words in this section reissue the invitation of 11:7 ("But let us go to him"). The needs of Lazarus and the occasion for the manifestation of God's glory supersede the threat of Judea.

The introductory section of the Lazarus story closes in verse 16 with Thomas' words to his fellow disciples, "Let us also go, that we may die with him." Thomas is the paragon of loyalty here, offering to follow Jesus even to the point of the disciples' own death. This loyalty has an ironic undertone, however, given the subsequent words of Thomas in the Farewell Discourse (14:5-7) and his obstinance in the face of the resurrection (20:24-25). Thomas is ready to follow Jesus, although the full weight of his own words is unknown to him. When the hour of death finally comes, he will fall away (16:32). In Thomas' closing words, the evangelist brings together both 11:7 and 15—let us go to Judea, where they are trying to kill Jesus (v. 7), and let us go to Lazarus who is dead (v. 15). It is unclear to whom Thomas refers when he says, "that we may die with *him*"—Lazarus or Jesus. In the context of this narrative, however, a clear and absolute distinction is unnecessary, because the end result is the same regardless of what antecedent is assumed. Jesus goes initially to Lazarus' place of death, but he goes ultimately to his own (11:2, 4).

On the Way to the Tomb
Verses 17-27, Jesus and Martha

In verses 17-19 the reader's attention is redirected to the family who has suffered loss and who grieves. These verses recall the opening verses of the chapter. Verses 1-2 function to set the drama of life and death in the specific context of one particular family. The focus shifts in verses 7-16 to include the disciples, but verses 17-19 remind the reader that this is still a family stary. The action of this narrative may have wide-ranging implications (11:4), but its immediate impact is felt in the midst of a grieving family. God enters into the most intimate, unassuming, and fragile places of our lives.

Three additional aspects of verses 17-19 deserve mention. First, with Jesus' arrival in Bethany, the journey silently hoped for by Mary and Martha and finally initiated by Jesus is at an end. Note the precise description in verse 18 of Bethany's location, with its explicit mention of Jerusalem. Jesus is only two miles from the city in which they have tried to kill him and in which he will die. Second, Jesus' words of verse 14 are now elaborated upon in the narrative: Lazarus has been in his tomb for four days already. Popular Jewish belief held that the soul remained near the body for three days after death, so the reference to four days, one day more than the required three, removes any doubts about Lazarus' death.[3]

Third, it is important to note that Mary and Martha do not mourn alone. Many Jews had come to them, in order to join them in mourning. The Jews of verses 19 are not the Jewish antagonists we find in chapter 9,[4] but are Jewish men and women who come to offer their presence in consolation and support to these two Jewish sisters. The family does not mourn alone, because their community mourns with them.

The story moves forward against this backdrop of mourning and Lazarus' four-day entombment. What we find next, perhaps to our surprise, is that Jesus still does not proceed directly to

Lazarus' tomb. The act of the raising of Lazarus may be our focus as we approach this story, but it is not so singularly the Fourth Evangelist's focus. The family's grief and Lazarus' long entombment do not cause Jesus to rush to the tomb. Instead, as verses 20-37 show, Jesus lingers with the family, conversing with them. The Fourth Evangelist devotes much time and care in preparation for the raising of Lazarus, so that when Lazarus does walk out of the tomb, the reader will be able to understand the significance of the act and to see the glory of God in that act. The time that the Fourth Evangelist takes in bringing Jesus to Lazarus' tomb contains an important warning for the preacher. The preacher of this text ought not to arrive at Lazarus' tomb any faster than Jesus does.

When word of Jesus' arrival reaches the two sisters, Martha comes to Jesus first (v. 20). The dialogue between Jesus and Martha has much in common with the other Fourth Gospel lessons we have examined, but especially with John 4. As we study the give and take between Jesus and Martha in these verses, we will frequently hear echoes of Jesus' conversation with the Samaritan woman.

Martha's words to Jesus open with two bold statements:
(1) Lord, if you had been here, my brother would not have died (v. 21);
(2) Even now I know that whatever you ask from God, God will give you (v. 22).

Martha's words are an odd combination of accusation and affirmation, of resignation and expectancy. Her words lament Jesus' absence and perhaps negligence, while at the same time affirming her faith in Jesus' ability to act. Martha's words in verse 21 echo Jesus' words in verse 15. In verse 15, Jesus stated that for the disciples' sake, he was glad he was not *there*. Martha states that if he had been *here*, Lazarus would not have died. Martha and Jesus interpret Jesus' absence differently, but both are aware that Jesus' absence and Lazarus' death are intimately connected.

Verse 22 boldly asserts Martha's confidence in Jesus' ability to evoke God's presence and aid. When the two sisters sent word of Lazarus' illness to Jesus, they never explicitly asked him to do anything, but verse 22 now articulates Martha's desire for Jesus to act on Lazarus' behalf. The precise meaning of the phrase "even now" is unclear. Martha's words and deeds in the rest of the story (see especially v. 39) indicate that she does not actually envision that Jesus will bring Lazarus back to life, but the "even now" of verse 22 does suggest that even in the face of death, Jesus will be able to act. Martha's words are a confession of trust in Jesus' power "even now" to mobilize God for good.

Martha's words have communicated her trust in Jesus and her hope-filled conviction that Jesus will know what to ask God. In verse 23 Jesus speaks directly to Martha's hopes: "Your brother will rise again." These words to Martha are brief and to the point, but as the remainder of the dialogue will show, they are deceptively straightforward. How this verse is understood (and misunderstood) is pivotal in establishing the dynamics of the rest of the chapter and in signaling what is at stake in the raising of Lazarus.

Martha responds to Jesus' words affirmatively. She couches her agreement with him in the language of traditional Jewish teachings on the resurrection: "I know that he will rise again in the resurrection at the last day." In our discussion of John 9, we noted the importance of being attentive to how and when different characters use the verb "know." Frequently what a character asserts he or she knows is an obstacle to the perception of what is really true. Martha's use of the verb "know" in verse 24 is no exception. She interprets Jesus' words through her own preconceived categories and assumptions, and so is confident that she understands and agrees with what Jesus says about the resurrection. Verses 25 and 26 demonstrate, however, that the distance between Martha's understanding and Jesus' words is great.

Jesus' response to Martha immediately challenges such traditional eschatological categories and expectations. Jesus, by his very presence, has made such traditional modes obsolete: "I am the resurrection and the life." The victory over death that the resurrection represents is present "even now," incarnate in the person of Jesus. Jesus, who transforms all categories, ultimately transforms even categories of life and death. Nothing remains outside the sphere of Jesus' transforming power. By identifying himself as both the resurrection and the life, Jesus identifies himself as lord over the present power of death and the future power of death. In vivid poetic language, Jesus breaks out of the categories within which Martha wants to contain the possibilities of life. By the shattering of those categories, Jesus makes available and enacts new life possibilities that did not exist prior to this narrative. The preacher, through the interpretation of this text, must make these new life possibilities present for the congregation in the same way that the narrative makes them present for the reader.

Jesus' first response to Martha, then, is christological. His second response is soteriological: "he who *believes in me*, though he die, yet *shall he live*, and whoever *lives* and *believes in me shall never die*" (italics added). These verses consist of two parallel phrases built around three main verbs: believe, live, and die. In verse 25b, the focus is on the effect that believing in Jesus has on death:

believes in me/dies⸻► yet lives.

In verse 26a, the balance is reversed, and the focus is on the effect believing in Jesus has on life:

lives/believes in me⸻► never dies.

The hinge of both verses, the only piece that remains constant, is the expression "who believes in me." Verses 25b and 26a thus make a radical claim for the power of faith in Jesus: Believing in Jesus transforms death (v. 25b), believing in Jesus transforms life (v. 26a). These verses play out the poetic language of verse 25a and give body to the ways in which Jesus reorders life and death. Faith is the point of access to the resurrection and the life made available in Jesus.

The verb "believe" is picked up in Jesus' final question to Martha: "Do you believe this?" Verses 25 and 26a make it clear that the question Jesus asks is not idle curiosity, but is a fundamental question of life and death. When Jesus asks Martha if she believes, he is asking her whether or not she is to be included among those of whom he has just spoken. He is offering her the chance to have her life transformed.

Martha, who has earlier demonstrated her trust in Jesus (v. 22), responds to his question affirmatively: "Yes, Lord; I believe that you are the Christ, the Son of God, he who is coming into the world." Martha responds with a stream of christological titles, all of which have resounded elsewhere in the Fourth Gospel (see especially 1:35-51). One must pay careful attention, however, to the difference between what Jesus asks Martha and the content of her response. Much like the Samaritan woman in John 4:25, Martha's response is couched in traditional categories that reflect traditional Messianic expectations. Her words neither reflect nor embrace the life-giving newness of which Jesus has just spoken. Martha confesses her belief in Jesus, but because of the gap between Jesus' radical poetic language and her own tradition-bound language, the question of whether or not Martha's confession is adequate lingers. The story will wait awhile before giving the answer to that question.

Verses 28-37, Jesus and Mary

In verse 28 the focus of attention shifts away from Martha to Mary. Martha returns from her conversation with Jesus and summons her sister Mary for him. When Mary rises and goes to Jesus, she greets him the same way her sister did: "Lord, if you had been here, my brother would not have died." This repetition of Martha's words by Mary has led critical scholarship to raise many questions about the relationship between the Mary and Martha pericopes, in particular about which pericope can lay greater claim to authenticity and priority in the tradition.[5] Such questions, while important for their contributions to our understanding of how the Gospel traditions were shaped in their transmission, are not particularly helpful in regard to preaching the text. They lead us away from the canonical form that is the basis of our proclamation. When we think about the Mary pericope in the context of Lenten preaching, avenues of thought other than those of source criticism will be more fruitful.

First, while it can be argued that the exchange between Mary and Jesus does not greatly advance the plot of the story,[6] this pericope does serve an important function in the overall context of John 11. The words of Martha that Mary repeats reemphasize the connectedness between Jesus and Lazarus' death. Mary, like her sister before her, explicitly links Jesus' absence and Lazarus' death. To the two sisters, Jesus is not a detached, objective bystander, but someone who could have played a decisive role on behalf of Lazarus. Before the story is over, Jesus will indeed play that decisive role, and his presence will then be as explicitly linked to Lazarus' life as his absence now is to his death.

Second, when Mary goes to Jesus, she does not go alone. The Jews who are consoling her go with her, thinking that she is heading to her brother's tomb to weep. The conversation between Mary and Jesus, unlike Martha's conversation, is not a private conversation, but one witnessed by all Mary's fellow mourners. The connection she makes between Jesus' absence and Lazarus' death is no longer a private confessional statement, but becomes the property of all those who are gathered. Mary's words, therefore, despite their repetitiveness, do add something to the story. They provide the Jewish mourners with the insight necessary to share in the central claims of the narrative.

Mary also does one thing that Martha does not do—she falls at Jesus' feet and weeps. Mary and those Jews with her bring their grief and lay it before Jesus. Their weeping and grief have a remarkable effect upon Jesus. When he saw their weeping, "he was deeply moved in spirit and troubled." This response of Jesus is extremely problematic to interpret. The simplest reading of verse 33 would be to say that Jesus joins Mary and the others in their grief, but the two verbs used to speak of Jesus here will not allow such a reading.

The first verb (*embrimaomai*), translated by the Revised Standard Version as "deeply moved," occurs only in the Lazarus story in the Fourth Gospel (11:33, 38) and infrequently elsewhere in the New Testament (Matthew 9:30; Mark 1:43; 14:5). In its non-Johannine occurrences, the verb is associated neither with mourning nor grief, but occurs in contexts of reproach and rebuke. Nothing, therefore, argues for a softening of these verses into a romantic reading of Jesus' emotions and sympathy. Instead the verb *embrimaomai* must be read as more closely akin to anger and consternation. The second verb used in verse 33, *tarassō*, reinforces this interpretation, because its primary sense is that of disturbance (cf. John 5:7; Acts 15:24, 17:8; Matthew 2:3).

If we understand Jesus' reaction in verse 33 as one of anger (the King James Version may be most helpful in its translation of this verse—"he groaned in the spirit, and was troubled"), the question needs to be asked: Why does the weeping of Mary and her companions provoke him to anger and distress? It has been argued that Jesus is angry because of their lack of faith.[7] Such a reading does not fit the context, however, and indeed contradicts one of the central claims of the story, because Jesus' gift of life is so radical that no one, no matter how faithful, could be expected to have anticipated it. A more convincing and compelling answer is that which dates back to the earliest interpreters of the church—that Jesus is angry and distressed because of the evidence of the power of death in the world.[8] The tears of the mourners remind Jesus of how much of the battle with death remains to be fought. Such a reading will not contribute to our portrait of the compassionate, empathetic Jesus, but it does function to remind us of how seriously Jesus took his vocation.

Out of this moment of grief and consternation, Jesus turns his attention to Lazarus. Now, thirty-four verses into the story, Jesus finally inquires about the whereabouts of Lazarus' body. In verse 11 Jesus told his disciples that he was going to Judea to awaken Lazarus from sleep, yet since his arrival in Bethany, Jesus has been more preoccupied with the two sisters than with the dead and buried Lazarus. That Jesus turns toward Lazarus' tomb only after he has been present to both sisters may suggest that the lifegiver's real offer is to the "living," not to the dead (cf. Luke 20:38).

The exchange between Jesus and the mourners about the location of Lazarus' body is important. Jesus asks where they have laid Lazarus. In 20:15 Mary Magdalene will say to Jesus, whom she mistakes for the gardener, ". . . tell me where you have laid him."[9] Jesus' question thus anticipates Mary's later request, and another connection between the story of the raising of Lazarus and the story of Jesus' death and resurrection is made. One story can be heard echoing in the other.

The mourners' response to Jesus also contains echoes of other Johannine texts. Their words, "Come and see," recall Jesus' first meeting with his disciples in chapter 1. When two of Jesus' first disciples ask Jesus where he is staying (1:38), his response to them is "Come and see" (1:39). In the John 11 text, this invitation to "come and see," first offered by Jesus, is offered to him. This echoing reflects a frequent pattern in the Fourth Gospel, in which a statement made or question asked by Jesus is later directed to him (cf., for example, 1:38; 4:27; 18:4; 20:15, where the repeated question is "what do you seek?"). The invitation to come and see is critical to the dynamics of faith in the Fourth Gospel (cf. also 1:46; 4:47), and there is a certain irony in that invitation here. The mourners invite Jesus to come and see Lazarus' tomb, but they have no idea what will actually take place at the tomb. They are in truth the ones who have to "come and see."

Jesus weeps in response to the crowd's invitation (v. 35). Some of the crowd take Jesus' tears to be a sign of his grief at the death of someone he dearly loved. The reader could accept the crowd's words as the correct reading of Jesus' tears, but several things argue against it. First, Jesus' weeping in verse 35 occurs in the context of verses 33 and 38, where Jesus' reaction, as we have noted, is more that of anger and rebuke than tender grief. The Fourth Evangelist has already signaled the reader that Jesus' reactions are not to be read simply through human analogies. Second, in the Fourth Gospel the crowd is never the most reliable interpreter. The crowds continually misunderstand Jesus' words (e.g., 6:41-44, 52-59) and Jesus' identity (7:25-29, 40-44). John 12:27-29 provides the most helpful warning against placing too much confidence in the crowd's understanding of the event. In that pericope, God's voice speaks to Jesus from heaven, but some of the crowd think it is thunder and others think it is an angel. The reader should therefore be leery of immediately accepting Jesus' tears as a sign of his grief.

The most convincing argument against accepting verse 36 as the normative interpretation of Jesus' tears is that the crowd cannot agree among themselves. As in chapter 9, where Jesus' deeds engender a split response, Jesus' weeping engenders a split reaction here. Some in the crowd take Jesus' tears as a symptom of his impotence in the face of serious illness and death: "Could not he who opened the eyes of the blind man have kept this man from dying?" With these words, the mood of the crowd has changed. No longer are the Jews who gather with Mary and Martha simply fellow mourners come to share in the sisters' grief. Instead they begin to resemble all the other crowds in the Fourth Gospel who question Jesus, who long for signs, who doubt Jesus' power and identity. The words of this skeptical group make an important contribution to the story. They make explicit the connection between the healing of John 9 and the Lazarus story, a connection the reader has sensed implicitly since verse 4. There is indeed a connection between the gift of sight and the gift of life. The question is, will the crowd—and the reader—be able to embrace the connection?

At the Tomb
Verses 38-44

In verse 38 Jesus finally arrives at the tomb. We traditionally refer to John 11:1-53 as "the raising of Lazarus," yet the actual raising of Lazarus occupies precious little time in the telling of the story. Only seven out of forty-four verses of the text take place at the tomb, and the raising of Lazarus is accomplished in two brief verses (vs. 43-44). The Fourth Evangelist has devoted thirty-seven verses to introducing the miracle, in order to establish the appropriate interpretive categories for the reader. In chapter 9, most of the evangelist's interpretive work followed the miracle; here it precedes it. When Jesus arrives at the tomb, deeply moved by the power of death, the reader knows that the one who stands at the mouth of the tomb is not any common miracle worker. The one who stands at the mouth of the tomb is the resurrection and the life.

The cave in which Lazarus is entombed is sealed with a stone. Jesus orders the stone to be removed (v. 39). In John 20, when Mary Magdalene arrives at Jesus' tomb, the stone will already be removed from the opening. When Mary arrives, the power of death has already been vanquished. At Lazarus' tomb the power of death is still in force. The tomb is still sealed, and Jesus must intercede in order to open the tomb to life.

Martha tries to stop Jesus, however. Martha, who we last heard confessing that Jesus is the Christ, reappears on the scene. Notice carefully the manner in which Martha is identified: Martha, the sister of *the dead man*. Martha is not identified in relation to her living sister, Mary, nor even to Lazarus by name (cf. vs. 5, 28), but is identified only through her relation to a dead man. This detail underscores the reality of Lazarus' death and the centrality of that death for the scene that is about to be played out. The power of death can dominate life, even to the point of defining Martha's identity.

In our discussion of verses 25-26, we noted the distance between Jesus' question and Martha's answer. Jesus asked her if she believed that he was the resurrection and the life, and she had answered him with traditional Messianic affirmations. The reader was left with lingering questions—Was Martha's confession adequate? Was her understanding adequate? Martha's response to

Jesus in verse 39 now answers these questions, and the answer is a resounding "no." Martha attempts to prevent Jesus from opening the tomb. She presents Jesus with the logical and biological reasons against opening the tomb, much as Nicodemus in chapter 3 mustered all kinds of arguments to speak against being born *anōthen* (3:4). Martha tries to stop Jesus, because what he wants to do contradicts all known categories of order, all known categories of life and death. Martha protests because she is defined by death and lives in its power. No one would be foolish enough to open the tomb of a man four days dead. No one, that is, except Jesus.

Jesus will not be deterred by Martha's protestations. His words to her confirm that Martha's previous confession was inadequate: "Did I not tell you that if you would believe you would see the glory of God?" As in chapter 9, believing and seeing are once again linked. Martha has confessed her faith (v. 27), but her faith categories were inadequate to comprehend the radical offer of life, the manifestation of the glory of God in Jesus. From the opening verses of the chapter (11:4), Jesus has linked Lazarus' death with the glory of God, but these words have been passed over by both his disciples and Lazarus' family and friends. They have no frame of reference through which to interpret what Jesus offers. Now, at the tomb, these words can be passed over no longer. In a very succinct phrase ("so they took away the stone"), the reader learns that Jesus' will wins out, that Martha's protests will not be credited. The glory of God will be seen. The power of death at work in Martha is not powerful enough to resist the disclosure of glory.

The stone is taken away, the tomb is open—the moment for action has come. Once more, however, the Fourth Evangelist works against the reader's expectations. At this most critical and dramatic moment, the Fourth Evangelist slows down the movement of the narrative. Instead of directing his attention to Lazarus' tomb, Jesus lifts his eyes to God. The content of Jesus' prayer is troubling at first glance. His words suggest that this is not a genuine prayer, but a "show" prayer, prayed for the benefit of the assembled crowd. Such an interpretation misreads the text, however. Jesus does pray out loud so that those around him can hear, but it is not an act of bragging or boasting. It is rather a speech act that gives concrete embodiment to the Father/Son relationship that dominates the Fourth Gospel (cf. 3:34-35; 10:30; 12:49; 14:24). In John 17, on the eve of his Passion, Jesus also turns his eyes heavenward and prays. Both moments of prayer (cf. also 12:27-28) declare that Jesus is not alone. At Lazarus' tomb, as also later at his own Passion, Jesus' prayer makes readily apparent whence his ability to give life comes (cf. 5:21, 26).

In verse 43, after he has prayed, Jesus cries out to Lazarus, "Lazarus, come out." The cry is loud and intense enough to assault the bonds of death (note especially the use of the verb *kraugadzō*). The groaning of verses 33 and 38 (KJV) is now brought to speech. The verb *kraugadzō* also establishes another connection between the Lazarus story and the Passion narrative. When Jesus enters Jerusalem in chapter 12, the crowd will cry out when they meet him (12:13). Jesus will be greeted by cries again before the Gospel narrative ends (18:40; 19:6, 12, 15). In those contexts, however, in ironic contrast to Jesus' cry at Lazarus' tomb, the loud cry is uttered to summon death, not to assault it, because the people cry out (*kraugadzō*) to crucify Jesus.

Jesus' cry not only assaults the bonds of death—it shatters them. Lazarus comes out of the tomb in response to Jesus' cry (just as Jesus will enter the tomb in response to the people's cry). The raising is accomplished by a word, by calling Lazarus by name. In John 20, when Mary is in conversation with the "gardener," the critical turning point will also come when Jesus calls her by name (20:16, cf. 10:3). The wording of verse 44 is very important: "The dead man came out, his hands and feet bound with bandages, and his face wrapped with a cloth." Even though Lazarus is now alive and walking, he is still identified as the "dead man." (Cf. the frequency with which the man born blind is referred to as the "blind man" in chapter 9 even after he has received his sight.) The identification of Lazarus as the dead man underscores two things. First, it keeps before the reader exactly what Jesus has done—he has made a dead man live—and second, it distinguishes the raising of Lazarus from Jesus' own resurrection. The risen Jesus will never be identified as the "dead man."

The details about the burial cloths also distinguish this raising from the resurrection of Jesus. Lazarus comes out of the tomb still bound in his death clothes, and Jesus must give additional commands (v. 44b) to free Lazarus from his bindings. At Jesus' resurrection, the disposition of the burial cloths is quite different. The Fourth Evangelist devotes two verses of chapter 20 (vs. 6-7) to describing the precise location of the linen cloths in the tomb. The Lazarus story is particularly helpful in understanding these problematic verses. Unlike Lazarus, Jesus emerges from the tomb unfettered by the bonds of his burial. Lazarus is a dead man, who lives again by virture of the saving words and presence of Jesus. The burial cloths are a reminder of his dependence and mortality. By contrast, all the old signs of death are left behind by Jesus. Not even the clothes of death have any claim on him.

In the Lazarus story, we have a stupendous, world-shattering gift of life. A man, dead, is called out of the tomb and walks out alive. Yet this act in and of itself is not the "point" of the story. The narrative has offered many clues about how properly to interpret this raising, so that we should not be misled by surface impressions:

—it is for the glory of God (11:4)
—that the Son of Man may be glorified (11:4)
—that if you believe, though you die, you will live (11:25)
—that if you believe, you will see the glory of God (11:40).

The raising of Lazarus is an act that defies categorization, that offers life only as it shatters preconceived categories. Martha and Mary are pious, devout believers, family friends beloved of Jesus, yet even they are not prepared for the fullness of Jesus' offer of life. The only categories that can contain the events of John 11 are these: I am the resurrection and the life (v. 25).

This analysis of John 11 has attempted to demonstrate the importance of *how* the story is told, not just *what* the story tells, and to probe the implications of that for preaching. In John 11, the Fourth Evangelist does not merely *tell* the reader that "the Son gives life to whom he will" (5:21), but *shows* the reader what it means to speak of Jesus as the one who gives life. Jesus' power over death is not restricted to 11:43-44, but is present throughout the narrative as Jesus breaks open the death-dealing categories according to which the disciples, Mary and Martha, and the Jews attempt to live. In this text, the Fourth Evangelist has created a narrative world in which the reader can experience Jesus as the resurrection and the life. The preacher is called to recreate that astonishing world for the congregation.

The greatest wonder of this text may be that despite Mary and Martha's inability to understand what Jesus is about and to grasp fully what he has to offer, *Jesus offers life anyway.* To those who are open, to those who grieve, to those who know there is nowhere else to turn, to those who will risk the experience of being transformed by Jesus, Jesus offers life. "Lazarus, come out," he says, and out walks a man known to be dead, four days in the tomb. The dead man lives. The old order no longer reigns. We see the glory of God.

The Epilogue
Verses 45-53

The story is not over yet, however. In many ways, the most difficult part of the story has just begun. The epilogue poses a troubling question: How do we respond to this gift of life? Many of the Jews who mourn with Mary see and believe (v. 45), but some go and tell the Pharisees what Jesus has done (v. 46). They go and tell those who know and who attempt to control knowledge that their well-ordered world is under attack. This latest announcement about Jesus is more than those who have so much at stake, who have so much to lose, can handle. Jesus has given life, he has concretely demonstrated his radical gift of life—and the efforts of the chief priests and Pharisees to kill him intensify (vs. 47-53). The gift of life leads to death.

In one of the most widely recognized instances of irony in the Fourth Gospel, Caiaphas prophesies regarding Jesus' vocation and mission (vs. 49-50).[10] His words are an urging to rid the people of Jesus, but his words ultimately say much more than he intends. As the Fourth Evangelist's commentary points out (vs. 51-52), Caiaphas did not intend to speak of the salvific power of Jesus' death, but his words had a mind of their own.[11] In the face of Jesus, prophecy, too, cannot be controlled and managed for a utilitarian end.

This Lenten reading ends on a most ominous note: "So from that day on they took counsel how to put him to death" (v. 53). The wording of this verse leaves no doubt but that the raising of Lazarus is the catalyst for the renewed desire to kill Jesus. In 12:9-11, the raising of Lazarus becomes a catalyst for the decision to kill Lazarus as well. In chapter 9 the religious authorities wanted to deny the miracle of sight by denying the identity of the man born blind. The gift of sight is dangerous. The gift of life in chapter 11 is that much more dangerous, and so the attempt is made to destroy all evidence of the gift, not merely to deny it. The hostility of the powers is evoked by the shattering of categories.

The gift of life, then, leads to death. From 11:53 on in the Fourth Gospel, the focus is unflinchingly on the Passion of Jesus. The world could not allow such a radical transformation of categories, such a radical gift of life, to dwell in its midst. A frequent refrain in the Fourth Gospel is the world's hatred for Jesus and his followers (7:7; 15:18-19; 17:14). The world hates Jesus because it is being dismantled by the power of life that he offers. The world, therefore, has only one option—to kill the giver of the gift before the world is called into question again. The world's protests may also be our protests: I do not want my world turned upside down. I want to be perfectly sure that I know up from down, life from death, that I remain in control of the ordering of my life. The world says, "Lazarus will rise again, but on the last day, *not on this day.*" The authorities took counsel how to put Jesus to death in an attempt to turn this amazing gift of life into a virtuoso act. The world would countenance such a radical act once, but no follow-up acts will be allowed. The world would isolate the act from its on-going interpretive danger.

The world did not understand, however, the world that could not—or would not—let go of its own well-defined categories enough to be open to the transforming experience of Jesus. The world that would die for what it knows and controls really did not know at all. The knowledge and understanding that pass such a world by is this: The gift of life is not stopped by death. The world longed to stop the gift of life, but the life-giver of John 11 does not operate according to what the world wants. The narrative of John 11 has demonstrated that. The reader has been turned and re-turned and re-formed by John's story of Jesus. Whenever we want to grab hold, to control, Jesus surprises us again. The gift of life will not be stopped by death.

Conclusion
"Do Not Hold Me"
(John 20:1-18)

It is the first day of the week. Mary Magdalene is at the tomb quite early, while it is still dark. She sees that the tomb is opened, that the stone has been rolled away (cf. 11:39, 41), and she runs to tell Peter and the disciple whom Jesus loved. Mary is confused and perplexed because, "They have taken the Lord out of the tomb, and we do not know where they have laid him" (v. 2). Those whom Jesus encountered during his life were quick to point out and defend what they knew. They insisted upon what they knew, even when it blinded them to what Jesus had to offer (cf. Nicodemus in John 3 and the Pharisees in John 9). But now, in the aftermath of Jesus' death, we have a freely given confession of "we do not know" (v. 2). The events of Jesus' death have made all confident pronouncements of knowledge obsolete. A new epistemology is required.[1] The comfortable categories of certitude have been shattered by the resurrection.

Simon Peter and the beloved disciple come and go from the tomb (vs. 3-10), and now Mary is back at the tomb, alone and weeping. She stoops to look into the tomb, and sees two angels sitting where Jesus' body should have been, where it had been laid on the day of his death. The angels ask Mary, "Woman, why are you weeping?" She answers them with the same words she spoke earlier to Simon Peter and the beloved disciple, "Because they have taken away my Lord, and I do not know where they have laid him." Mary's words, however, are more personal when she speaks to the angels: "my Lord"; "I do not know." It is her world that is affected by the radical disjunction of this empty tomb.

Mary's tears are not simple tears of mourning (cf. 11:33), however, but tears of confusion, consternation, and amazement. She is crying because nothing is known. All the certitudes have failed:

(1) Jesus should be in the tomb where the angels sit, but he is not.

(2) They laid him in this tomb (19:42), but now he is gone.

(3) Mary came to the tomb to grieve, but the object of mourning is missing.

Like the disciples in John 4 who assumed that Jesus' food came from another human source (4:33), Mary assumes that Jesus' disappearance can be traced to a human agent ("they have taken him away"). Mary stands at the mouth of the empty tomb, before two angels, but she cannot see. She can only see what makes sense according to her system of logical possibility, and so the mystery of the empty tomb is domesticated.

When Mary finishes speaking to the angels, she turns around and sees Jesus (cf. Exodus 16:10). As the narrator very intentionally tells the reader, however, "she did not know that it was Jesus" (v. 14). Mary is much like the Samaritan woman in John 4—Will she be able to recognize who it is that is speaking to her? (4:10). Mary does not know two things—where Jesus is and with whom she speaks. As the narrative unfolds, we will see that when she discovers one unknown, she will have discovered the other.

Jesus asks Mary two questions: "Woman, why are you weeping? Whom do you seek?" (v. 15). Jesus' first question is the same as that of the angels, but his second question moves beyond theirs. His second question reveals that Jesus already knows why she is weeping, because he knows that she seeks someone who is missing. These two questions are the first words spoken by the risen Jesus in the Fourth Gospel. The question "Whom do you seek?" reiterates the first words spoken by Jesus in the opening chapter of the Fourth Gospel, "What do you seek?" (1:38). The ones who first meet Jesus during his life and ministry are asked what they seek; the one who first meets the risen Jesus is asked what she seeks. The Fourth Evangelist's intentional framing of the Fourth Gospel narrative with these questions of invitation cannot be overlooked. This question of invitation is still the governing question for all who enter this text.

Mary's ignorance of Jesus' identity is emphasized by the narrator's words, "supposing him to be the gardener" (v. 15). She is in conversation with the one whom she seeks, with the one for whom she weeps, but she does not see him. She does not see Jesus because she knows that "they have taken him away." She does not see Jesus because she does not really seek him. She seeks a missing corpse, not a risen Lord. To seek anything other than a missing corpse would be sheer foolishness, sheer irrationality, sheer impossibility. Mary sees and knows in the ways the world has taught her to see and know, and so she sees only a gardener, not Jesus (cf. the sight of the man born blind and the Pharisees in John 9).

Mary speaks bluntly to the "gardener": "Sir, if you have carried him away, tell me where you have laid him, and I will take him away" (v. 15). The irony in Mary's words is rich. If she knew to whom she was speaking (cf. 4:10), her request would be unnecessary. Mary expresses the same ignorance that was expressed by many who encountered Jesus during his life and ministry, ignorance of the "where to" and "where from" of Jesus.[2] This scene in the garden is a concrete narrative embodiment of that ignorance and blindness. Even in the face of the risen Jesus, Mary must still ask "where" and "who."

Jesus speaks only one word in response to Mary's request: He calls her by name (v. 16a). When Mary hears her name, she turns to Jesus again (cf. v. 14), but this time her turning is one of recognition. He has addressed her; she addresses him, "Rabboni" (v. 16b). What Mary did not see she now sees; what she did not know she now knows. Mary did not see Jesus when she was listening to the voice dictated by the ways of the world, the voice that told her that if Jesus' body was missing, someone must have taken it. When she listens to Jesus' voice, however, when she hears Jesus call her by name, she is no longer bound by the world's possibilities and impossibilities. Jesus' voice breaks through the ways of the world and Mary knows who it is that speaks with her. She knows where her Lord is.

In chapter 11, Jesus' voice brings Lazarus out of the tomb. Jesus' voice breaks through the power of death and makes new life possible. The power of Jesus' voice to break through to new life is prefigured in the parable of the shepherd in 10:1-6. Lazarus in his tomb and Mary at Jesus' tomb recognize the voice of the shepherd. Jesus calls them by name; they are his (cf. Isaiah 43:1). The false voices of the thieves and robbers will no longer be heeded, because only one voice leads to life.

Jesus' next words to Mary are somewhat puzzling: "Do not hold me, for I have not yet ascended to the Father; but go to my brothers and sisters and say to them, 'I am ascending to my Father and your Father, to my God and your God'" (v. 17).

Critical scholarship has drawn attention to the questions this verse raises about the Johannine understanding of the ascension.[3] For our purposes, however, it will be more helpful to put those particular questions on hold and focus instead on Jesus' two commands to Mary:

(1) Do not hold me.
(2) Go tell my brothers and sisters.

In their immediate context, Jesus' first words to Mary ("do not hold me") can be read as a caution not to interfere with God's plan: Do not hold me, because I am now ascending, and if you hold me, I will not be able to return to the Father. Verse 15 shows that Jesus' caution was not misplaced. Mary said to the "gardener," "tell me where you have laid him, and *I will take him away*" (italics added). The events at the tomb were not proceeding according to expectations, and Mary wanted to take control and return events to "normal." To return events to "normal," however, is to return things to human control, i.e., to "hold" Jesus.

The Greek verb for "hold" is *haptō* (middle, *haptomai*), which means "to touch, hold onto, cling."[4] The expression "do not hold me," therefore, has connotations of physical holding, but also communicates a broader range of meaning. To hold onto something is to control, to own, to define, to manipulate, to manage, to co-opt for one's own ends. Jesus is not rebuffing Mary with his words in verse 17, but is teaching her the first post-resurrection lesson: Jesus cannot and will not be held and controlled.[5] Not even the "pangs of death" can hold Jesus (cf. vs. 6-7; Acts 2:24).

Throughout John 3, 4, 9, and 11, we have seen examples of people "holding" Jesus. Nicodemus "held" Jesus as a particular teacher from God, the Samaritan woman "held" Jesus as a particular Messiah, the Pharisees "held" Jesus as a sinner, Martha "held" Jesus to traditional eschatological expectations of life and death, present and future. In all four texts that we have studied, new life was offered only when Jesus broke free of such attempts to hold and manage him. In 20:17 Jesus says directly what all four narratives have demonstrated and embodied: "Do not hold me."

Jesus cannot be contained or identified through our labels and categories.[6] To do so is to limit to our notion of the possible the impossibilities Jesus offers. Jesus will neither be known by nor serve our self-interests (cf. John 9), our definitions of the possible and impossible (cf. John 3), our hopes and fears (cf. John 4 and 11). The confession of the Samaritan townspeople (4:42), the confession of the blind man (9:38), the miracle wrought at Lazarus' tomb (11:43-44), all demonstrate that we come to know who Jesus is only when we allow Jesus to be Jesus and stop holding him to who we want him to be.[7] If we define Jesus according to our hopes instead of allowing Jesus to embody God's hopes, we will never know what it means to be born *anōthen* (3:3).

Jesus' concluding words in verse 17 make this clear. Jesus sends Mary to be a bearer of news, and the content of that news is critical (cf. Isaiah 52:7). His words are words both of fulfillment and promise: "I am ascending to my Father and your Father, my God and your God." The fulfillment is that what has been foreseen and promised throughout the Fourth Gospel (e.g., 7:33; 8:14; 16:28) is now a reality: Jesus goes to the Father. This fulfillment carries with it a new promise for the disciples, however, in that a new relationship with God is initiated. "My Father" is now "your Father;" "my God" is now "your God." Jesus has made a transformed life with God a reality for the disciples. That for which Jesus prayed (see John 17, especially verses 11, 21-26) is coming to pass. The disciples, now Jesus' brothers and sisters, can share in the impossibilities of God's hope.

Jesus offers sonship and daughtership with God (cf. Romans 8:14-17), provided that *he is not held.* Jesus' words of caution and promise in verse 17 are closely interrelated, because we risk losing the promise if we hold Jesus to what we think he should be. If we hold Jesus, then Jesus is our slave and not our brother (v. 17). If Jesus becomes our slave, then full access to God is lost. It is the Son, not the slave, who makes God known (1:18); it is the Son, not the slave, who sets us free (8:36). To hold Jesus is to lose our only chance for life.

Mary goes to the disciples and says, "I have seen the Lord" (v. 18). Mary's words are the core Easter proclamation, and they bring this pericope to a conclusion. In verse 2 Mary ran to the disciples, announcing, "I do not know where the Lord is." In verse 18 she announces, "I have seen the Lord." Jesus called Mary by name, and she is moved from consternation to proclamation. Jesus showed her that one is no longer required to see with the eyes of the world, and she is moved from weeping to joy. Jesus promises her and her brothers and sisters a new life with God, and she is moved from despair to hope.

The Easter Sunday text of 20:1-18 provides a powerful conclusion to the Lenten texts we have studied. In those texts we have been led to an experience of Jesus that transcends our expectations and transforms all our categories. The texts of John 3, 4, 9, and 11 have made Jesus present to the reader. The invitations offered to the characters in those texts have been offered to the reader as well. The Johannine texts that form the heart of the Lenten lectionary for Year A are truly Lenten preparatory texts. Each one of them leads us closer to the confession, "I have seen the Lord." Each of these texts affords the preacher and the congregation the chance for a fresh experience of Jesus.

Like most of the characters in these texts, we live in a world in which our best efforts are put into managing, knowing, ordering, and controlling. Such efforts, like those of most of the characters in these texts, leave us hopeless and fatigued, because they depend on our own resources and systems, our own interests and definitions. The Jesus who meets us in John 3, 4, 9, and 11 announces the end of such a world and such efforts at holding. The Jesus who invites us to him in these texts offers resources for life and health that are not available until he offers them. The Jesus who beckons us in these texts creates new possibilities out of the defeat of our own impossibilities. He creates a new world in which we are called to live, the only world in which new life is possible.

What Jesus offers in these texts is entrusted to the preacher to offer in the sermon. The challenge is not to "hold" Jesus in our sermons, but to allow our proclamation to be remade by the power and presence of Jesus embodied in these texts. If we listen to these texts carefully and allow them to shape our preaching, then we have a chance to turn and see not the gardener, but Jesus. We have a chance to join Mary in moving from weeping to joy, from despair to hope, from death to life.

Notes

Introduction

1. Fred B. Craddock, *Overhearing the Gospel* (Nashville: Abingdon, 1978), powerfully captures the issues involved in preaching to people who have already heard.
2. This understanding of the Bible obviously speaks against the most celebrated recent instance of summary, *The Reader's Digest Bible*, ed. by Bruce M. Metzger (Pleasantville, NY: The Reader's Digest Association, 1982).
3. For a full discussion of the relationship between the narrative mode of a text and its theological claim, see Gail R. O'Day, *Revelation in the Fourth Gospel: Narrative Mode and Theological Claim* (Philadelphia: Fortress Press, 1986).

Chapter One

1. The precise endpoint for the dialogue between Jesus and Nicodemus is difficult to determine. The central interpretive problem is whether to include verses 16-21 as part of the dialogue or not. I have decided not to include verses 16-21 in my analysis because they seem to function as an independent discourse rather than as an integral part of the Nicodemus text. While many of the themes of 3:1-15 do continue into verses 16-21, this second discourse seems to function more as an epilogue. For a different view of the relation between 3:1-15 and 3:16-21, see Raymond Brown, *The Gospel According to John*, vol. 29 (Garden City, NY: Doubleday and Company, Inc., 1966), pp. 147-149.
2. Nicodemus is frequently understood as an example of a "crypto-Christian," Jewish Christians who are afraid to confess publicly their belief in Jesus. So, e.g., M. de Jonge, "Nicodemus and Jesus," *BJRL* 53 (1971) 337-359. Raymond Brown, *The Community of the Beloved Disciple* (New York: Paulist Press, 1979), pp. 71-73, gives a full discussion of crypto-Christians, but does not place Nicodemus in that group. See J. Louis Martyn, *History and Theology in the Fourth Gospel*, Second Edition (Nashville: Abingdon, 1979), for a discussion of crypto-Christians and ways in which the tension between Jews and Christians relates to the purpose of the Fourth Gospel.
3. In Jeremiah 37:16-21, King Zedekiah requests a similar night visitation with Jeremiah. Zedekiah's night visit to Jeremiah contains the same elements of tension as Nicodemus' visit. For a discussion of Jeremiah 37:16-21 and its relation to John 3, see Walter Brueggemann, *The*

Creative Word (Philadelphia: Fortress Press, 1982), pp. 41-46.

4. See, for example, the recent study of American Christian fundamentalism by Eric W. Gritsch, *Born Againism* (Philadelphia: Fortress Press, 1982).

5. The double meaning, "from above" and "again," is possible only in Greek. There is no Hebrew or Aramaic word with a similar double meaning. See Raymond Brown, *The Gospel of John*, p. 130.

6. It is, of course, quite difficult to capture the double meaning in any translation. That means that explicit and intentional interpretive work must be done when preaching and teaching this text. If preference is given exclusively to one translation of *anōthen* over another, either to "from above" or "again," then the richness of the text is lost. Ways to communicate the ambiguity of *anōthen* in English must be worked at.

7. For a seminal discussion of the function of the narrative complexities in the Nicodemus story, see Wayne A. Meeks, "The Man from Heaven in Johannine Sectarianism," *JBL* 91 (1972): 44-72.

8. Walter Brueggemann, "'Impossibility' and Epistemology in the Faith Tradition of Abraham and Sarah (Genesis 18:1-15)," *ZAW* 94 (1982): 615-634, discusses the power of God's possibility as a central assertion of biblical faith.

9. The basic analysis of world construction is by Peter Berger and Thomas Luckmann, *The Social Construction of Reality* (Garden City, NY: Doubleday and Company, Inc., 1966). For the construction of world through story, see Amos N. Wilder, "Story and Story-World," *Interpretation* 37 (1983): 353-364.

10. For a discussion of irony in the Fourth Gospel, see Paul Duke, *Irony in the Fourth Gospel* (Atlanta: John Knox Press, 1985) and O'Day, *Revelation in the Fourth Gospel*.

11. Meeks, "Man from Heaven."

Chapter Two

1. For an overview of the relationship between Jews and Samaritans and how it pertains to John 4, see John Macdonald, *The Theology of the Samaritans* (London: SCM Press, 1964).

2. Henri J.M. Nouwen, *Creative Ministry* (Garden City, NY: Doubleday and Company, Inc., 1971), discusses the value of one's openness to interruptions and breaks in the routine (the "itinerary") for an obedient and creative ministry. Jesus is the model of such openness for Nouwen.

3. For a more detailed structural outline and exegesis of John 4, see O'Day, *Revelation in the Fourth Gospel*, chapter 3. Birger Olsson, *Structure and Meaning in the Fourth Gospel* (Lund: G.W.K. Gleerup, 1974), also provides an in-depth interpretation of John 4.

4. The Fourth Evangelist appears to be drawing on the Jacob traditions in Genesis 33:19; 48:22, and Joshua 24:32 in these verses. See Jerome H. Neyrey, "Jacob Traditions and the Interpretation of John 4:10-26," *CBQ* 41 (1979): 419-437, and "The Jacob Allusions in John 1:51," *CBQ* 44 (1982): 586-605.

5. For a discussion of the rabbinic prohibitions, see C.K. Barrett, *The Gospel According to St. John*, Second Edition (Philadelphia: Westminster Press, 1978), p. 240. Samuel Terrien, *Till the Heart Sings* (Philadelphia: Fortress Press, 1985), p. 132, sees Jesus' intentional violation of societal conventions here as a demonstration of the inclusivity of Jesus' ministry.

6. Rudolf Schnackenburg, *The Gospel According to John*, Vol. I, trans. by Kevin Smyth (New York: Crossroad, 1982), p. 426.

7. Wayne A. Meeks, *The Prophet-King. Moses Tradition and the Johannine Christology* (Leiden: E.J. Brill, 1967), p. 38, identifies the irony of this question. See also the discussion of 9:29 below, p. 111.

8. The tradition that Jacob miraculously produced water from a well is not present in the Old Testament, but developed in later rabbinic literature. See José Ramón Diaz, "Palestinian Targum and the New Testament," *Novum Testamentum* 6 (1963): 76-77, and the Neyrey articles cited in note 4.

9. E.g., Brown, *The Gospel of John*, p. 170; Barrett, *John*, p. 234; Olsson, *Structure and Meaning*, p. 180. For a more detailed discussion of the irony of this verse, see Duke, *Irony in the Fourth Gospel*, pp. 70, 94; R. Alan Culpepper, *Anatomy of the Fourth Gospel* (Philadelphia: Fortress Press, 1983), pp. 172-176; and O'Day, *Revelation in the Fourth Gospel*, ch. 3. The irony of this verse is repeated in 8:53, when the Jews ask, "Are you greater than our father Abraham?"

10. For the relationship between Second Isaiah and the Fourth Gospel, see D.R. Griffiths, "Deutero-Isaiah and the Fourth Gospel," *ET* 65 (1953-54): 355-360, and F.W. Young, "A Study of the Relation of Isaiah to the Fourth Gospel," *ZNW* 46 (1955): 215-233.

11. Walter Brueggemann, *Hopeful Imagination* (Philadelphia: Fortress Press, 1986), chapters 5 and 6, provides a powerful discussion of the language and images of hope in Second Isaiah.

12. For a review of the history of scholarship of these verses, see Francis J. McCool, "Living Water in John," in *The Bible in Current Catholic Thought*, ed. by J.L. McKenzie (New York: Herder & Herder, 1962), pp. 226-233.

13. The most blatant example of this approach to verses 16-19 is found in the recent book by Paul Duke, *Irony in the Fourth Gospel*. Duke refers to the woman as a "five-time loser" (p. 102) and a "tramp" (p. 103). Such judgments, however, are not made on the basis of the text itself, and reveal more about the interpreter's biases than about the

Fourth Gospel.

14. Edwyn Clement Hoskyns, *The Fourth Gospel*, ed. by F.N. Davey, Second Edition (London: Faber and Faber, Ltd., 1947), pp. 237, 243 suggests that the woman wants to determine at which sacred place she should pray for forgiveness of her sins that Jesus has brought to light. Duke, *Irony in the Fourth Gospel*, p. 103, says that the woman tries "desperately" to put distance between herself and Jesus. So also Robert Kysar, *John* (Minneapolis: Augsburg Publishing House, 1986), p. 66. Brown, *John*, p. 176, doubts whether "a Samaritan woman would have been expected to understand even the most basic ideas of the discourse." In all of these interpretations, the woman is given very little credit as a legitimate conversation partner for Jesus.

15. This tension between God's free presence and God's fixed presence can be seen clearly in the narrative of the dedication of the temple in 1 Kings 8. The narrator of 1 Kings saw clearly that the danger in determining a fixed location for God's dwelling is that God will be managed and controlled by those who manage the location. The Johannine Jesus speaks against the same danger.

16. Through the images of wind, fire, and the moving wheels in Ezekiel 1, the book of Ezekiel communicates imaginatively and powerfully God's freedom to move and hence, God's freedom from human control. Of that powerful vision, the prophet writes, "Such was the appearance of the likeness of the glory of the Lord" (Ezekiel 1:28).

17. This verse is of particular interest for John 4, since both Samaritans and Jews value the traditions of Moses.

18. Other absolute uses of the "I AM" saying include 6:20; 8:24, 28, 58; 13:19; 18:6. For a discussion of the Johannine use of "I AM," see Rudolf Bultmann, *The Gospel of John* (Philadelphia: Westminster Press, 1971), p. 225, no. 3, and Philip Harner, *The "I Am" of the Fourth Gospel* (Philadelphia: Fortress Press, 1970).

19. See, e.g., Kysar, *John*, p. 68.

20. Terrien, *Till the Heart Sings*, p. 133, identifies the woman's role here as that of an apostle, one who is sent.

21. George W. MacRae, S.J., "The Fourth Gospel and *Religionsgeschichte*," *CBQ* 32 (1970), p. 23, observes that ". . . as long as one tries to grasp Jesus as a Jew or a Greek or a Gnostic would, [one] both succeeds and fails, for Jesus is the fulfillment of all these expectations, but he is caught up in none of them." John 4 shows that one could easily add Samaritan expectations to MacRae's list.

22. For an example of a sermon informed by the give and take of John 4, see Eloise Hally, "Lent III," in *Women of the Word*, ed. by Charles D. Hackett (Atlanta: Susan Hunter Publishing, 1985), pp. 37-41.

Chapter Three

1. See, for example, George W. MacRae, *Invitation to John* (Garden City, NY: Image Books, 1966), p. 124.

2. Paul D. Duke, *Irony in the Fourth Gospel* (Atlanta: John Knox Press, 1985), p. 119.

3. In verse 14, the name "Jesus" appears, but the name is used by the narrator in his commentary. The name of Jesus is not spoken by any of the characters in the story.

4. J. Louis Martyn, *History and Theology in the Fourth Gospel*, Second Edition (Nashville: Abingdon, 1979), p. 30 and *passim*, has articulated the two levels on which John 9 operates. The first level is the witness to a particular event during Jesus' lifetime; the second is the witness to Jesus' "powerful presence" in the particular events experienced by the Johannine church. These two levels speak to the question of absence and presence.

5. Matthew and Luke do not take over this healing story in their use of the Markan tradition, and the earthiness of the healing method is one reason frequently advanced for the omission of the story.

6. For a suggestive discussion of the relationship between Bartimaeus' blindness and his social marginality, see Walter Brueggemann, "Theological Education: Healing the Blind Beggar," *The Christian Century* 103 (1986): 114-116. Brueggemann's comments on the Bartimaeus story also speak to the man born blind in John 9.

7. In verses 13-17, 40, the central antagonists of the story are called the "Pharisees." In verses 18-23, they are called the "Jews." (In vs. 24-34 they are never identified with a noun.) The variation in nouns is not evidence of different sources. Martyn's suggestion is more likely correct—that the switch to the "Jews" so late in the chapter reflects the situation and concerns of the Johannine community (*History and Theology*, pp. 27, 32-33).

8. Verse 22 is the critical verse in Martyn's analysis of chapter 9. Martyn carefully and convincingly discusses the threat of being cast out of the synagogue as reflective of the life situation of the Johannine community. See *History and Theology*.

9. Rudolf Bultmann, *The Gospel of John* (Philadelphia: Westminster Press, 1971), p. 336, no. 1.

10. For a discussion of verbs of knowing in the Fourth Gospel, see James Gaffney, S.J., "Believing and Knowing in the Fourth Gospel," *TS* 26 (1965): 215-241.

11. These words of the man born blind have come down to us in the hymn, "Amazing Grace,"

> I once was lost, but now am found,
> Was blind, but now I see.

The use of these words in that hymn captures what the Fourth Evangelist wanted to communicate—the gift of sight is an act of God's grace (v. 3).

12. Wayne A. Meeks, *The Prophet-King. Moses Tradition and the Johannine Christology* (Leiden: F. J. Brill, 1967), p. 38. See also the discussion, above, of 4:11.

Chapter Four

1. For an overview of the critical discussion of the relation of the Lazarus story to the Synoptic tradition, see Raymond Brown, *The Gospel According to John*, Vol. 29 (Garden City, NY: Doubleday and Company, Inc., 1966), pp. 427-430.

2. For the meaning of *sodzō*, see *BAGD*, p. 798. Donald Senior, C.P., *The Passion of Jesus in the Gospel of Mark* (Wilmington, Delaware: Michael Glazier, Inc., 1984), p. 120, makes a similar observation about the use of *sodzō* in Mark.

3. André Neher, *The Exile of the Word* (Philadelphia: The Jewish Publication Society of America, 1981), p. 24, provides a particularly helpful reflection on this Jewish belief.

4. See chapter 3, footnote 7, above, for evidence of the flexibility with which the Johannine tradition uses the term "Jews." The word is used on many occasions simply to indicate ethnicity or religious orientation (e.g., 4:22), with no sense of antagonism or hostility.

5. For an overview of the critical discussion of the question of priority in the traditions of Martha or Mary, see Rudolf Schnackenburg, *The Gospel According to St. John*, Vol. 2 (New York: Crossroad, 1982), pp. 319-321.

6. See, e.g., Brown, *John*, p. 435.

7. See Bultmann, *John*, p. 406.

8. Chrysostom, in his interpretation of this verse, makes this suggestion. John Calvin, in his commentary on John, also supports this view.

9. For a full discussion of Mary's question, see Paul S. Minear, "'We Do Not Know Where . . .' John 20:2-2," *Interpretation* 30 (1976): 125-139. See also our concluding chapter.

10. For comments on the irony of this verse, see, e.g., C.K. Barrett, *The Gospel According to St. John*, Second Edition. (Philadelphia: Westminster Press, 1978), p. 405, and Duke, *Irony in the Fourth Gospel*, pp. 87-89.

11. In Numbers 22-24, we find another example of an unsuccessful attempt to control the power of prophecy.

Conclusion

1. For a discussion of the current epistemological crisis, see Lesslie Newbigin, *The Other Side of 1984* (Geneva: World Council of Churches, 1984). For a discussion of the Gospel of John as a paradigm for a new epistemology, see Jose Miranda, *Being and the Messiah* (Maryknoll, NY: Orbis Books, 1973).

2. Paul S. Minear, "'We Do Not Know Where . . .' John 20:2," *Interpretation* 30 (1976): 125-139. More generally, see Wayne A. Meeks, *The Prophet-King. Moses Tradition and the Johannine Christology* (Leiden: E.J. Brill, 1967), p. 38. See also our discussion of John 4:11 and 9:29.

3. The particular focus of critical debate is the relationship of crucifixion, resurrection, and ascension in the Fourth Gospel. See Raymond Brown, *The Gospel According to John*, Vol. 29a (Garden City, NY: Doubleday and Company, Inc., 1970), pp. 1011-1017. See also Godfrey C. Nicholson, *Death as Departure. The Johannine Descent-Ascent Schema*, *SBLDS* 63 (Chico, California: Scholars Press, 1983).

4. *BAGD*, p. 102.

5. See the discussion of this scene in Samuel Terrien, *Till the Heart Sings* (Philadelphia: Fortress Press, 1985), pp. 136-137. Terrien focuses on the physical connotations of the verb "hold," but arrives at a similar conclusion to the one reached here: "The holy always requires distance."

6. In a recent essay published in *The New York Times Book Review* (Vol. XCI, no. 12), Andrew Greeley provides a contemporary articulation of the Johannine understanding of Jesus:

> The only real Jesus is one who is larger than life, who escapes our categories, who eludes our attempts to reduce Him to manageable proportions so that we can claim Him for our cause. Any Jesus who has been made to fit our formula ceases to be appealing precisely because He is no longer wondrous, mysterious, surprising. We may reduce Him to a right-wing Republican conservative or a gun-toting Marxist revolutionary and thus rationalize and justify our own political ideology. But having done so, we are dismayed to discover that whoever we have signed on as an ally is not Jesus. Categorize Jesus and He isn't Jesus anymore. (p. 3)

7. In the Old Testament, Ezekiel demonstrates a similar understanding of God. The holiness of God will not be co-opted for human purposes. On John and Ezekiel, see Bruce Vawter, "Ezekiel and John," *CBQ* 26 (1964): 450-458. On Ezekiel's insistence on the freedom of God, see Walter Brueggemann, *Hopeful Imagination*, chapters 3 and 4.